Cheap Chow

Kenneth Lo was born in Foocho
Universities of Peking, Cambrid
of physics, from which he chang
England. During his time in this country he has pursued a wide variety of careers and activities. He has been a diplomat, fine-art publisher, industrial relations and welfare officer (with Chinese seamen in Liverpool), journalist, lecturer, professional tennis player, and now food critic and cookery writer.

He has written several books on Chinese cookery. His *Quick and Easy Chinese Cooking* is also published in Pan.

Apart from writing about Chinese cookery, he lectures widely on the subject, and talks and demonstrates occasionally on television. He has for several years been the Chinese food consultant to the Consumers' Association, and is at the moment adviser on Chinese food to several major food concerns both here and abroad.

Also by Kenneth Lo in Pan Books
Quick and Easy Chinese Cooking

Kenneth Lo

Cheap Chow

Chinese Cooking on Next to Nothing

illustrated by Delia Delderfield

Pan Books London and Sydney

First published in Great Britain 1976 by
Elm Tree Books Ltd in association with
Pan Books Ltd
This edition published 1977 by Pan Books Ltd,
Cavaye Place, London SW10 9PG
3rd printing 1980

ISBN 0 330 25199 6
Printed in Great Britain by
Richard Clay (The Chaucer Press) Ltd, Bungay, Suffolk

Contents

Measurements and metrication

The weights and measures used throughout this book are based on British Imperial standards and the nearest workable metric units to keep the recipes in the right proportions.

International measures

Measure	UK	Australia	New Zealand	Canada
1 pint	20 fl oz	20 fl oz	20 fl oz	20 fl oz
1 cup	10 fl oz	8 fl oz	8 fl oz	8 fl oz
1 tablespoon	$\frac{5}{8}$ fl oz	$\frac{1}{2}$ fl oz	$\frac{1}{2}$ fl oz	$\frac{1}{2}$ fl oz
1 dessertspoon	$\frac{2}{5}$ fl oz	no official measure		
1 teaspoon	$\frac{1}{5}$ fl oz	$\frac{1}{8}$ fl oz	$\frac{1}{6}$ fl oz	$\frac{1}{6}$ fl oz

Conversion of fluid ounces to metric

4 tablespoons ($2\frac{1}{2}$ fl oz) = 70 ml (0·7 dl)
2 tablespoons ($1\frac{1}{4}$ fl oz) = 35 ml
1 tablespoon ($\frac{5}{8}$ fl oz) = 18 ml
1 dessertspoon ($\frac{2}{5}$ fl oz) = 12 ml
1 teaspoon ($\frac{1}{5}$ fl oz) = 6 ml
(all the above metric equivalents are approximate)

Equivalents

1 UK (old BST standard) cup equals $1\frac{1}{4}$ cups in Commonwealth countries
4 UK tablespoons equal 5 Commonwealth tablespoons
5 UK teaspoons equal 6 New Zealand or 6 Canada or 8 Australia teaspoons
1 UK dessertspoon equals $\frac{2}{3}$ UK tablespoon or 2 UK teaspoons

In British cookery books, a gill is usually 5 fl oz ($\frac{1}{4}$ pint), but in a few localities in the UK it can mean 10 fl oz ($\frac{1}{2}$ pint)

Other non-standard measures include:
Breakfast cup = approx 10 fl oz; tea cup = 5 fl oz;
coffee cup = 3 fl oz

Foreword

In the summer and autumn of 1974, when I was writing *Cheap Chow*, I was acting as founder of the Chinese Gourmet Club in London, consultant in Chinese food to the *Good Food Guide*, to Marks & Spencer, and general adviser on the U.K. market to several Chinese firms. These activities necessitated my eating at least a couple of ten-course banquets every week, and generally dining off the fat of England's green and pleasant land. Every Monday evening during this period however, I would join my friend, Mr Robert Li, for a one-dish dinner which he would cook in his Hampstead bed-sitter, where he has lived for nearly four decades. Being in part-time acting, he was frequently short of funds and had to make do with what there was on hand. This was often very limited indeed. There were occasions, I remember, when there was neither tea, coffee nor beer and we had to resort to drinking hot water, which reminded me of similar situations in North China many a long year ago, where hot or warm water was often a beverage for the common people. Yet Mr Li always cooked with both pride and relish, and the dish he produced was often the best and most enjoyable one I had during the whole week. I often reflected on this irony. As time went on, I could not but come to the conclusion that the poor really missed very little of the gastronomic delights indulged in by the bloated rich, and that the important thing is, principally, to know what is good food (in China we had the expression 'Chih Wai', to describe a person who has a feeling for good food and good flavour) and be prepared to take the care and trouble to bring out the qualities inherent in food. This has nothing or very little to do with the cost of ingredients or elaborate preparation. The recipes in this book are selected with these thoughts in mind, and I am dedicating the book to all those who can enjoy 'good flavour' without pretension and to all the people in China who are today at least adequately if not enjoyably fed, and not subjected to the extreme privation that they have been subjected to throughout history.

K. H. C. Lo, 1975

Introduction

When confronted with the problem of having to produce food cheaply and in some bulk (cooking in some bulk for five or six persons is always cheaper than cooking piecemeal) one should naturally turn to such populous countries as China and India where millions have had to live on a near-starvation diet for millennia and yet survive in considerable strength: China with her present population of 800 million and India with hers of 500 million. The Chinese and Indian experiences are particularly enlightening because these are not only populous subcontinents but also centres of great cultural traditions, and nobody can deny that food preparation is one of the most fundamental of a people's cultural traditions and expressions.

The Chinese experience in this sector of human activity is particularly relevant because of the inherent flexibility of China's liberal food tradition and the sheer range of Chinese dishes, which seem to make use of everything edible. During the past two or three decades it has been proved that Chinese food (or the way we Chinese treat ordinary food materials) from the point of view of taste alone is appealing to all kinds of people's palates throughout the world, whether they be Scots, Yorkshiremen, Nigerians, South Americans or Japanese. I was quite startled once when I was invited to give a lecture in Greenock on Chinese food and cooking. After arriving at Glasgow Central station I had to trek out by local railway towards the seaport. On arrival it took me quite a time to locate the meeting place. Never having been there before in my life, Greenock appeared to be very dark and deserted on that December evening. For all practical purposes, the place could have been a Chinese provincial town in the mid-twenties! I began to wonder if anybody would be there to attend my lecture. But, when I stepped into the lecture hall, I was completely bowled over by seeing over four hundred people in the audience, patiently sitting there to await and greet my arrival!

On another occasion, I was invited to give a lecture on Chinese food and cooking in the Winter Garden in Eastbourne. Eastbourne is, as everybody knows, a very different kind of place from Greenock; here the audience consisted mostly of well-to-do people who were members of a literary society, who were used to attending lectures which were cultural and uplifting in their content. I had expected the attendance to be in the region of fifty to sixty people, and wondered why the organizers had booked the Winter Garden. The number of people who actually came to the lecture was 750!

The experience of these two lectures, and of scores of others, has proved to me that the appeal and interest of Chinese food and cooking are quite universal. When it comes to the palate and stomach, there seems to be no class barrier or distinction: Chinese food and cooking seem to appeal equally to the bourgeoisie, the aristocrats and the proletarians!

The particular relevance of Chinese food and cooking to people who are interested in producing cheap foods lies in the fact that the production of Chinese food is normally based on the theory of what I have often called 'exploding savouriness'. By this is meant that we start with only a small amount of meat (or fish or fowl), with soya sauce and one or two strong vegetables (ginger, onion, garlic), which together produce a highly savoury mass of food. This is then, in turn, cooked with three to five times its quantity of vegetables, thus rendering the meat and vegetables together into a much greater mass of savoury food. When this larger savoury mass is eaten with four to five times its own weight of bulk food (rice, pasta, steamed buns, pancakes or toasted buns, etc.) the ultimate quantity of edible food thus produced will probably be in the region of ten to fifteen times the initial weight of meat employed.

So it is quite feasible in Chinese cooking to use no more than, say, 225 gr ($\frac{1}{2}$ lb) of meat, to start with, to feed six or seven people quite satisfactorily, almost like a 'nuclear explosion', with the meat used as the original 'detonator'. What is interesting in this approach to cooking is that in the process of 'explosion' the other ingredients in the cooking (the vegetables, etc.) all help to add to the consumers' intake of minerals and vitamins, which are essential to human health. The only things that might be lacking in the Chinese diet are milk and cheese. But, today, these can easily be added, when required, without much expense. The Chinese diet is as healthy as any. For almost all so-called advanced countries of the world are today also overweight countries. A little more kosher approach to food – where dairy produce is never consumed with meat – would be all to the good.

But for the majority of people who have taken to Chinese food, the most important thing about it is not so much that a good Chinese meal is well balanced in nutriments, but that it is good to eat – delicious and very satisfying. Yet, when you go into the intricacies and technique of Chinese cooking, you will find that we Chinese rarely use any flavouring agent not normally used in the average Western kitchen, apart from soya sauce, and the other by-products of soya bean, such as salted black beans, soya paste, soya jam (sweetened soya paste) and soya cheese. These, when employed in conjunction with the more normal seasonings and flavourings, such as salt, pepper, sugar, chilli, mustard, wine, vinegar, monosodium glutamate and a judicious use of oils (especially the more aromatic ones, such as sesame oil), combine to produce that potent savouriness which is inherent in Chinese cooking.

On the other hand, if you went more deeply into Chinese cooking you would find that much of its sophistication is derived not only from the use of flavourings, but by a deliberate exploitation of the elements of heat, texture and contrast between bland foods and savoury foods, as well as between well-cooked food and the sweet freshness in quick-cooked food. The combination of all these factors, and the judicious manipulation of their interplay in cooking, give Chinese cooking its preeminent position in the culinary world.

Even in 'Cheap Chow' these principles can be applied. In the main, the Chinese meal is built around the structure of the combination of savoury foods with bulk foods. This book will be structured on much the same principle; we shall have chapters on savoury foods sandwiched between chapters on bulk foods; the majority of these can be eaten to complement one another. There are also a number of cases where bulk foods and savoury foods are cooked together (as in pies, fried rice, etc), and therefore require no further foods to complement them. So the book will not be just about bulk foods, or 'food for fuel', but also about highly tasty and delicious foods. Indeed, many people who are used to expensive gourmet food have a preference for foods which are basic and wholesome, simply conceived and prepared.

Talking about 'food for fuel' reminds me of the Chinese expression, 'Chi Han', which means 'Hunger and Cold'. We always use the two words together, probably because in the old days we knew exactly what we were talking about: for hunger is most intense when accompanied by the threat of cold, and creeping cold is at its most unbearable when there is no food or prospect of food to come. However, this book is not only about the ways and means of using the long tradition and immense experience of Chinese food to appease hunger and relieve cold, but about doing so in such a way that the experience will be an enjoyable one.

Because of the Chinese preoccupation with hunger and cold, at least one item of the bulk food provided for a meal is hot, although some of the accompanying foods may be cold or only warm. For instance, when you are having congee or 'rice-gruel', which carries a large content of heat, the accompanying savoury items can be cold or just warm. Or if you are having cold-tossed noodles, or boiled flaked rice (whether in the form of fried rice or vegetable rice), or potato or bread, these are normally accompanied by a bowl of soup, which provides not only the necessary and useful liquid or 'savoury wash-down', but also the heat. Most people who have been cold and hungry will agree that one of the most effective and enjoyable ways of obtaining relief is to have a large bowl of substantial soup, accompanied by bread, toast, buns, rice, pasta or what have you.

In the Chinese concept, as I have mentioned before, bulk food is never eaten without the accompaniment of a savoury dish, or at least a dish or two of salted items or pickled foods.

On the level of 'food for fuel', pickled or salted items often feature largely in a Chinese meal; there is a need for something strong-tasting to counteract the blandness of the bulk foods. Even in times of semi-famine, Chinese peasants would still eat their bulk foods with some pickled or salted items, so long as they were not compelled to resort to consuming tree bark or roots of plants in order to exist – happily those terrifying old days are now over.

But even when one is still a long way from having to resort to tree bark and plant roots, one's attitude towards animal fats and skins will have undergone a sea change. In the past, 'drippings' of one sort or another have always been regarded as highly palatable food. In Chinese cooking, animal fat and skin are usually cooked to such a high degree of tenderness that they become, in effect, 'meat jellies', and when properly cooked are considered delicacies, prized by connoisseurs. They are particularly delectable when cooked with soya sauce and eaten with rice. Indeed, rice (in all forms) with soya-meat-gravy is often eaten with even greater appreciation than the meat itself. I shall endeavour to exploit this aspect of Chinese cooking to the full, for after all, meat-gravy is considerably cheaper than meat itself; and a mixture of meat, meat-with-fat-and-skin, and meat-gravy is something that the less wealthy of the West can learn to appreciate, to their advantage. Everyone knows that the choicest roast meat is only at its very best when the lean is interspersed with streaks of fat (and that pure lean meat is often quite insipid and tasteless). Proceeding from there, it is not such a distance to assume the Chinese approach of enjoying skin and fat.

People here already complain very loudly if their sugar or meat intake is reduced by a fraction. The real problem is more likely to be how to feed ourselves more cheaply or basically than we are accustomed to (which is to overfeed!) in large or small groups, or as individuals, if possible interestingly and enjoyably. The main point here is to see that the overall cost of food should, as a whole, remain in the region of about 50 per cent below the cost of a normal meal. This becomes somewhat easier when group feeding is involved – hence most of the recipes in this book are aimed at catering for five, six or seven persons, and when that makes too large a quantity of prepared food this can, in the majority of cases, be held over for a second or even third meal.

It should be noted that in Chinese food the savoury accompaniment is usually there to perform several functions: firstly to make the food more enjoyable, and secondly to provide the protein element, as well as some of the vitamins and minerals required in the human diet. Savoury accompaniments are normally prepared from meat (including fowl, fish and seafoods) or 'extensions of meat'. Their preparation uses the basic methods of Chinese cooking:

Red-cooking (or slow stewing in soya sauce)
'Lu', or cooking in 'master sauce' (which is used most frequently in cooking offal)
Stir-frying or quick stir-frying
'Assembling' (the assembling of different food materials and ingredients which may have been cooked and prepared in different ways)

In cooking and eating cheaply in the Chinese tradition the idea of making meat go further is naturally an important one. The concept falls in line with what I called earlier the 'nuclear explosion' theory of savoury food preparation. For this reason we Chinese are inclined to eat much larger quantities of vegetables than the average Westerners do in their normal diet. It may be that the best-balanced diet for the people of both East and West is for them each to assume and adopt something of the eating habits of the other: for the Chinese to consume more milk and dairy products, especially in their childhood and teens, and for the Western adult to eat many more vegetables.

Red-cooking

Coming back to the 'extension of meat', the methods used by the Chinese consist not only of cooking meat with vegetables, which are comparatively inexpensive, but also the widespread practice of cooking meat-gravy with vegetables.

One of the most popular forms of Chinese cooking, 'red-cooking' is simply slow stewing with soya sauce, and in the more refined instances, wine and sugar are added into the stewing, together with some herbs (e.g. anise, ginger), or tangerine peel. Very little water, if any, is added at the beginning, although a small amount may be added to the mixture towards the end. This produces a thick gravy, which is a great boon for using with all forms of bulk foods.

As already indicated, in this form of cooking the meat used need not be pure meat, but meat with bone and skin (such as knuckle or hand of pork, trotters, etc.). Gravy so produced is useful not only for eating with bulk foods, but also for cooking with and flavouring vegetables, which then become 'meat' – as far as we Chinese are concerned.

Using meat stock or broth

There is a cheaper way of producing meat-flavoured vegetables, which is to braise or stew them with meat broth or meat stock. Broth or stock can be easily produced in much greater quantity than gravy for a given amount of meat – or meat-bones and skin. When meat stock is cooked (braised for 6-10 minutes, or stewed for 20-30 minutes) with vegetables with some seasonings and fat added, it renders vegetables a highly appealing and savoury food, which can in turn be eaten with vast quantities of bulk food. Hence in China, cheap cuts of meat – such as the head, neck, feet, claws or carcase of poultry or animals (or even the head and bones of fish) – are used for just this purpose. Usually a given weight of such part of the animal produces at least four to five times its own weight of good meat stock. This can, in turn, be cooked with twice its own weight of vegetables, to produce a highly appealing mass of savoury food. The latter will then be consumed with enjoyment with at least two or three times its own weight of bulk foods. The total amount of 'food for fuel' that can be produced from, say, one lb of very indifferent meat should be in the region of 10-12 lb.

The recipes in the chapters on Vegetable stews and Soups are mainly based on this principle; 'soups' in these cases are largely diluted forms of stews. They can be made more interesting by the addition of some fresh ingredients (vegetables and others) a minute or two before serving. In some cases a small amount of aromatic ingredients is also added at the very last moment – such as sesame oil, freshly chopped chives or spring onions – to flavour the soup further. Small amounts of dried ingredients (such as shrimps) are often added at the initial stage, to give a new inflection to the general flavour. These touches lend sophistication to Chinese food, and are as applicable to Cheap Chow as they are to haute cuisine.

Cooking with 'master sauce'

In any country where there is a shortage of food, as there was in China, offal is much more extensively used and served than in the affluent West. The method generally used for cooking offal (as well as ordinary cuts of meat) is 'Lu' – to simmer in a 'master sauce' consisting largely of soya sauce, water, wine, sugar, herbs, dried vegetables and strong-tasting vegetables (such as onion, garlic and ginger). After making the master sauce the foods are simmered in it for ½–1½ hours, to lose the unwanted flavours that are peculiar to innards (or even that chemical taste that is associated with battery-produced fowls).

A master sauce is usually started by having a fowl, or a chunk of meat, which is cooked in soya sauce and bone stock for a good length of time and made characteristic by the strong participation of herbs, dried foods and strong vegetables.

Meats and other foods cooked in this manner are then usually taken out from the sauce and allowed to cool. When cold they are cut into neat slices or strips and served as 'Chinese hors d'oeuvres', or as accompaniments to rice-gruel (congee) at breakfast time, or to any bulk food. They are also very useful to nibble when drinking wine. When produced with care, these cold meats are highly regarded; they assume the position of prized delicacies. It is often the tradition of Chinese cuisine to promote foods such as sea-slugs, sharks' fins, 'birds' nests', and ducks' feet to 'delicacies' and price them at a much higher level than normal cuts of meat!

Not only meat items are cooked in the master sauce, but also eggs and hard vegetables. They would, of course, not require the same length of simmering in the sauce. Hard-boiled eggs need about 15-20 minutes and most hard vegetables 25-30 minutes. Vegetables so cooked are very appealing and palatable, partly on account of the flavour of the meat. The cooking of vegetables is often carried one stage further by having them 'cross-cooked' for a short period of time by 'quick stir-frying' with other vegetables or meats, which are sliced thin or shredded, together with other ingredients, similarly cut. In this way, the cross-flavouring of cooked foods with fresh foods, or dried foods, can often bring the orchestration of flavour blending to a new height.

'Stir-frying' or 'quick stir-frying'

This method of cooking probably accounts for the greatest number of dishes produced by the whole range of Chinese cuisine. 'Stir-frying' consists simply of stirring and cooking foods, which have been thinly sliced, shredded into matchstick or double-matchstick strips, or diced into small cubes, in a small quantity of oil (usually no more than 2-4 tablespoons), over a very high heat. The stirring and turning should be maintained throughout. Treated in this manner, the foods will generally be cooked within 2-3 minutes.

Timing is very important in this type of cooking: the harder foods, which require somewhat lengthier cooking, should be added into the hot or boiling oil first (even pork will cook easily in three minutes), and the items which only require shorter cooking last (such as shrimps, peas, diced chicken, etc.). Wine and other aromatic ingredients are usually added last, to cause the rise of a 'bouquet' which is pleasing to the nostrils. Because of the larger number of ingredients which can be blended into the cooking at different stages and with small additions of flavourings and seasonings the number of dishes which can be created out of the different 'orchestrations' is well nigh countless. The usefulness of 'stir-frying' in Cheap Chow recipes probably lies partly in the fact that various types of left-over foods can all be cut up and further stir-fried with other foods – fresh or cooked – to make a completely new dish in almost an instant. This is a style of cooking which is often favoured by restaurants, since there are usually quantities of left-over foods of one type or another, which can all be used up. Besides, in stir-frying, the cooking time required is minimal. Because of this extremely liberal tradition, Chinese catering establishments are usually much more efficient and profitable than any other known restaurants. One of the strengths of Chinese cooking is undoubtedly its ability to use up all the bits and pieces and convert them into a respectable dish in a few minutes.

'Assembling'

'Assembling' is a method of Chinese cooking that goes one step further than 'stir-frying' in combining and cross-cooking together ingredients, fresh, or cooked, or from different culinary backgrounds. Here a broth or stock is used as a unifying factor in a pot or casserole, where ingredients which perhaps have been deep-fried, stir-fried, braised, red-cooked, master-sauce-cooked, are joined with materials that may be poached, boiled, steamed, smoked, roasted, barbecued, dry-fried, or whatever. In other words, 'assembling' can be a grand conglomeration of ingredients, all from different backgrounds, and joined together in one pot. It is made more interesting by the addition of wine, fresh herbs, a drop or two of sesame oil or chilli oil (oil in which chilli pepper has been simmered).

The method of cooking is usually steaming: the foods and ingredients partly immersed in stock (which makes what we call a 'semi-soup' dish) are placed in a steamer to cook vigorously for a matter of 15-30 minutes. In the West, where not every kitchen is equipped with a steamer, the same end result can be achieved by assembling together all foods and ingredients in a heat-proof dish, and putting it into a pre-heated oven to cook for about 20-30 minutes. This period of cooking should be sufficient to seal the foods by binding them together into a characteristic unity, which tradition in this method of cooking requires.

A dish that is the product of 'assembling' can be as expensive or as cheap as one pleases. If expensive materials are used – and a great quantity of them can be incorporated – a very costly dish will result. On the other hand, if one is pressed for cash, 95 per cent of the ingredients put into the assembly can be vegetables, with the remaining 5 per cent divided between meat and dried foods (dried mushrooms are normally ten times more flavoursome than fresh mushrooms). Such an 'assembly', when picked up with a chicken stock cube, plus a minute quantity of wine added at the very last moment, can, though cheap, be very tasty indeed.

One ingredient that is frequently employed in assembled dishes is the Chinese transparent pea-starch noodle, which has the unusual quality of being able to absorb five to six times its own weight of soup or liquid without ever becoming mushy or soft in spite of prolonged cooking. It is therefore a very useful unifying element in such a dish.

Soups

When one's purse is pinched (or even when one feels flush) soups are always a very useful category of food to have around, to appease hunger or even simply to satisfy one's greediness. There is nothing like a hot, tasty bowl of soup to wash down any form of bulk food – say, bread and cheese.

In these modern times the habit of making soup is often lost because of the easy availability of canned or packet soup. Interest and nutrition in these manufactured soups is often minimal, if prepared and eaten purely on their own. Yet, from the flavouring point of view, they can be extremely useful. If a large stockpot could be kept simmering, with all the left-over vegetables, meats, bones and carcases, the resultant stock, when combined with manufactured soups, together with a small amount of freshly chopped meat or vegetables, and other selected ingredients, would always produce a soup that is not only nutritious but delicious enough for any connoisseur.

Soya sauce, curry and cheese

In Cheap Chow, where one cannot afford to indulge in using expensive materials in any quantity at all, flavouring is a matter of even greater importance than in *haute cuisine*, if one has not sunk to the level of indifference to the taste of the foods one eats. Luckily, the majority of flavouring agents are by no means expensive.

If there are three great flavouring ingredients in this world, they are undoubtedly soya sauce, curry and cheese. None of these three materials is essentially expensive, and by using them wisely and judiciously ordinary foods and materials can often be made so savoury and delicious as to put them on a par with gourmet foods. The later chapters in this book are devoted to inexpensive dishes that are prepared with the direct application of these three flavourings.

Curry is the principal flavouring matter of the whole subcontinent of India and Pakistan, where the number of dishes cooked with this indispensable ingredient must run into hundreds or thousands. With the spice trade having influenced Western palates during the fifteenth, sixteenth, seventeenth and eighteenth centuries, Western tastebuds are still very much attuned to highly spiced foods. Anyone who has taken to curry could hardly find a substitute (except for the highly spiced Chinese cuisine of the Upper Yangtze – those of Hunan and Szechuan – which have inexplicably become the rage of New York in very recent years).

As for cheese, its flavouring effect, and its beneficial influence on foods in general, is still probably underestimated by the ordinary run of cookery pundits. The sophistication of cheese seems to be in its regional varieties rather than in its application for flavouring. The subject probably deserves more individual study than has so far been given to it. Its use in Cheap Chow cooking can, in some instances, be crucial. The flavouring of cheese can probably be orchestrated into Chinese methods of cooking and flavouring. In this book we can only *touch* upon the use of cheese in Cheap Chow, in some cases in conjunction with Chinese methods of cooking.

The usefulness and benefits of soya sauce are now largely accepted throughout the world. But few people, even amongst professionals, realize the difference between using soya sauce in cooking and soya as a condiment (or dip), to be applied to foods on the table. In our case, I shall be writing about the application of soya sauce to foods in the raw and after they have been plain-cooked, which is an aspect of Chinese foods which is not given the attention it deserves.

Having surveyed these different aspects and general areas of our interest, let us launch ourselves into the dishes themselves, starting with rice.

1 Rice dishes

Congee or 'rice-gruel'

The closest Chinese equivalent to the Dickensian soup kitchen was the congee factory – congee, or rice-gruel, was the stuff which was ladled out in bowlfuls to the poor in China during times of famine, flood, drought, or any period of extreme shortages, which were perennial (especially during the winter) in all the centuries of the bad old past, before the People's Republic of China arose to wipe out the persistent nightmare, as recently as the 1950s. The cauldrons of steaming congee must have been a cheerful sight to millions of Chinese who were threatened not only by hunger but also by extreme cold. For congee is nothing if not warming. But what is congee, or rice-gruel?

Congee, or rice-gruel, is produced simply by boiling rice very slowly in 6-10 times its own weight of water. This is 4-6 times the water one normally uses in cooking ordinary boiled rice. For instance, in cooking boiled rice one would normally add $1\frac{1}{4}$ to $1\frac{1}{2}$ times its own volume of water, boil and simmer over very low heat for about 10-11 minutes, and then allow it to cook in its own heat under closed cover for a further 10 minutes (after turning the heat off), when a dry, flaky, but well-cooked rice should be obtained. This is the normal type of rice used in most

Chinese meals. Although simple to prepare, many Westerners are often recommended to adopt much more complicated processes, which frequently result in irretrievable complications. When cooking congee with 450 gr (1 lb) of rice, use 3-3·5 litres (5-6 pints) of water. To obtain good results, simmer over very low heat (putting an asbestos sheet under the pan is advisable) and cook for at least 1½-2 hours. The contents should be stirred fairly frequently. By the end of this slow cooking, the rice should have expanded by at least 5 to 7 times, producing sufficient rice-gruel to feed at least five or six people. Furthermore, if some flavourings are added to this rice-gruel (such as stock cubes and soya sauce and a little fat), it can now be consumed not only to appease hunger and relieve cold, but with considerable pleasure, particularly if supplemented with such salty, strong-tasting foods as pickles, salted or soya eggs, salted fish or meats, or soya cheese. Adding some vegetables to the rice-gruel during the later stages of its simmering – harder vegetables should be added earlier – produces a food that is not only enjoyable, but also well-balanced and nutritious.

The nutrition here can be easily increased by adding a small amount of roasted nuts (such as peanuts) during the very last minutes of the simmering, or the nuts can be placed in a small dish and eaten as an accompaniment to the congee. Two or three chicken stock cubes can also be added. In China, adding a teaspoonful or two of good quality soya sauce to the congee often provides all the interest it needs. This is frequently the diet of an invalid; when he has recovered slightly, an egg is broken into the congee to provide added nutrition.

On the other hand, connoisseurs enjoy the plain blandness of the congee itself, which seems to have a sweetness about it, especially when eaten with salty or highly flavoured foods. In average or well-to-do Chinese families, congee or rice-gruel is usually eaten at breakfast time. At that time of day it seems to fulfil two functions – that of fruit juices: to provide a refreshing effect; and that of Scottish porridge: to inject an early-morning inner warmth, so essential to those about to brave the winter chill outdoors.

In the past, congee was frequently eaten as a snack, or for

midnight supper (after their game of mahjong!) by better-off people in China. On such occasions the meal was usually made more interesting by the provision of some half a dozen dishes, which usually contain a selection of items: salt fish (crisp-fried), 'Thousand-Year-old Eggs' (eggs pickled and preserved in their shells in a mixture of mud and lime), roast salted peanuts, soya bean curd, soya cheese and 'soya meats' (cuts of meats, liver, kidney, tripe, intestines, tongues, etc., which have been simmered in a soya-based 'master sauce') plus one or two items of salted or pickled vegetables. This latter range of foods is usually quite inexpensive, especially as they are normally served in quite small quantities.

When it is necessary to lift such a meal from the basic to something a little more appealing, one need simply add a larger, usually red-cooked, meat dish, to eat with the congee.

In preparing congee (rice-gruel) in the West, with the purpose of maximizing the quantity of bulk food so as to feed the largest number of people, the method to follow is exactly the same as that used in China (see page 23).

Since it is the purpose of this book to cater for those who not only need 'food for fuel', but who also wish to *enjoy* eating when on short commons, we need to consider which of the best savoury accompaniments to congee are easily available in the West. Since these items need only be provided in small quantities – as savoury titbits to accompany several bowlfuls of rice-gruel – we need not be overwhelmed by their normal cost. Besides, these items need only be eaten cold, since bowls of congee represent masses of hot food and it is the tradition in China to eat them, more often than not, with cold, savoury, salted titbits.

Accompaniments to congee

Sardines go well with congee. An average-size canned sardine is usually sufficient with a large bowl of congee. Therefore, a can of sardines is enough to accompany 6-8 bowlfuls. Sardines are strong-tasting and highly savoury, which makes them ideal with congee.

Another good accompaniment to congee is smoked or salted

anchovy fillets. These can be taken in even smaller quantities than sardines because of their saltiness, which is accentuated by the bland, neutral but satisfying quality of rice-gruel. As in the case of sardines, which are often preserved in olive oil, the oil itself can be easily absorbed into the congee and – partly because of the sheer volume of rice-gruel that is being consumed – some 'lubricant' will often be welcomed.

In fact, all salted or smoked fish make ideal accompaniments for congee. The usual practice in coastal China is to fry (shallow-fry) salted fish over a low heat for 10-15 minutes, when they become quite crisp and aromatic and more intensified in taste. In such a state even a small morsel is able to go with several mouthfuls of congee. A piece half the size of a sardine can very well accompany a bowlful of rice. The eating of completely bland food (congee) with highly concentrated, tasty and flavoursome food (fried salted fish, etc.) has developed into such a tradition that even the wealthiest people would not feel that they were living well unless provided with some congee-with-accompaniments at some time in the course of the day.

Chinese accompaniments to congee

In China some of the types of food served with congee are:
'thousand-year-old eggs' (see page 25)
soya eggs
salted eggs
'meat wool' (lean meat which has been slowly stir-fried until it becomes completely dehydrated and resembles wool)
'soya meats' (meats that have been simmered in a soya-based master sauce: these include liver, kidney, tripe, intestines, pork, beef, trotters, etc.; the process is called 'Lu' – see page 16)
soya-bean curd and cheese
roasted and salted nuts
smoked meats and fish
Chinese sausages (like small salamis)
pickled vegetables, including turnips, carrots, greens, etc.
braised vegetables in soya sauce, including mushrooms, bamboo shoots, broccoli, etc.
'drunken' meats and seafood, including chicken, spare-ribs,

crab, prawns, etc. (these foods are immersed and marinated in wine after initial cooking)

Once again only a small quantity of each type of food is required (hence only saucer-sized dishes are used) and one can have as small or as large a selection as one pleases – dependent entirely on availability.

Cold hors d'oeuvres

It becomes apparent that nearly all the items that are normally served as hors d'oeuvres in the West are equally suitable accompaniments for congee. These include the following, used in small quantities:

anchovies and hard-boiled eggs
stuffed eggs
curried eggs
smoked beef, tongue, eel
smoked and salted herring
red cabbage or chou rouge (cabbage boiled in vinegar, drained and seasoned with oil, salt and pepper)
gherkins
mussels seasoned in oil, salt, pepper and vinegar
salamis and sausages of all types

Boiled rice

Rice is sometimes steamed in China, but this requires a longer period of cooking and therefore consumes more fuel; in the West, where few kitchens are equipped with steamers, it is probably more convenient to boil rice.

When cooked in quantity – 900 gr (2 lb) upwards, which should produce at least 2·25 kg (5 lb) of boiled rice – one should always bear in mind that heat at the bottom of the pan can be much higher than at the top, which can result in the rice at the bottom getting burned. Therefore, when cooking rice in some quantity it is always useful to use a heavy saucepan, or to place an asbestos sheet under the pan, or both. When you have got the necessary utensils, boiled rice should be one of the easiest things in the world to cook (although it is a subject which, for some strange reason, is riddled with controversy).

The easiest way to prepare boiled rice is to place the rice in a heavy pan with a fitting lid and add 1¼-1½ times its own volume of water, after having previously rinsed it under running water. Bring the contents to boil over high heat. When boiling begins, turn the heat to very low and insert an asbestos sheet under the pan. Leave the contents to simmer gently for ten minutes, then turn the heat off and leave the rice to cook in its own heat for a further ten minutes, when it should be ready. Do not open the lid at any time during the whole process of the cooking (least of all during the period when the rice is cooking in its own heat). When properly cooked, boiled rice should be dry and flaky.

Rice so cooked is the basic bulk food of China, which probably means that nearly half the people in the world are living on boiled rice for their daily diet. Rice is both dry and bland and, to be really enjoyed, should be eaten with soup and at least one savoury dish. Since soups need never be very expensive, and the savoury dish could consist of a 'red-cooked' meat dish, such a meal should not be beyond the means of anybody in the West who is used to eating one square meal a day. By this method, 675 gr (1½ lb) dry rice will yield 1·5-1·8 kg (3½-4 lb) cooked rice, sufficient for five or six people. At the current price such a meal should not cost more than £1, no more than 20p per head for a big, hearty meal.

Before we move on to explore the varieties of soups and savoury dishes that can be provided for such a meal, let us examine the several variations in which the basic boiled rice can be presented, although in China boiled rice is usually served plain. In the West, a good proportion of people are likely to enjoy rice more when it is cooked with some other materials or ingredients in it (e.g. kedgeree). In the Chinese tradition there are two types of rice dishes (rice as bulk food), where other ingredients are cooked and mixed in with the rice: vegetable rice and fried rice.

Fried rice

Fried rice is one of the major staple dishes served by the tens of thousands of Chinese restaurants in the West to their customers. It may be that as much rice is being fried up each day in the West as is being prepared in China, if only because 95 per cent of the time we Chinese eat our rice plain. Fried rice is by the nature of things somewhat dry (it should be dry and flaky and never soggy; hence it is often prepared from cold cooked rice) and is, therefore, best eaten with a soup. It is usually more savoury than, say, vegetable rice because fried rice usually contains eggs and a sprinkling of salted meats (ham, bacon, or salt-meats) and is flavoured with onion, which is the first ingredient to put into the pan to fry in the oil or fat. It may also contain almost any vegetable one can lay hands on but the vegetables will need to be diced into small cubes so that they can be cooked thoroughly during the very short time that is devoted to cooking this dish (1½-2 minutes). Green peas are the most convenient to use because they are just the right size for the purpose. Diced carrot can also be incorporated advantageously, for both its colour and its nutritional value. Tomato is another useful vegetable, for, apart from its attractive colour, when very lightly and quickly fried it adds a freshness of flavour that is very appealing. Small button mushrooms (the type usually supplied canned, or larger fresh ones diced to about 6 mm-1·25 cm or ¼-½ inch cubes) can be incorporated for their meaty flavour and texture. Some people have been known to use peanuts and raisins, but a taste for these is more Western than Chinese (although in *Cheap Chow* we are not primarily concerned with purity of origin; our concern is mainly with producing edible and appealing foods with a Chinese basis, inexpensively). Eggs seem invariably an integral part of fried rice, either hard-boiled and chopped, or as 'stir-fried' eggs, the latter being the Chinese version of scrambled eggs, where lightly beaten eggs are heated in a frying pan with a few tablespoons of oil or butter, broken up into 1·25-cm (½-in) pieces when they are about to set (and not vigorously scrambled up before the eggs have set as you normally do with scrambled eggs). When meats are used in fried rice – usually not much more than 25 gr (1 oz) per person – they should be liberally seasoned and stir-fried before being added to the rice and other ingredients. For their seasoning, either salt or soya sauce can be used. The comparative strength of the seasoning causes the meat to contrast sharply with the neutral blandness of rice. One of the unifying factors in fried rice is the oil or fat used in the stir-frying. The best results seem to be obtained by using oil (2-4 tablespoons) to fry the onions, ham, bacon and eggs, and butter (2-3 tablespoons) to stir-fry the vegetable ingredients. When they are hot and well-lubricated they are assembled in a finale of high-heat stir-frying together for a matter of 1-1½ minutes. When well cooked and immediately served, the ingredients are bound together by the heat and oil.

Well-prepared fried rice should be light, aromatic and hot. It should avoid being soggy, which happens if the rice used is too porridgy to start with (a situation which is almost irretrievable) or if too much stock, water or sauce is added during cooking. In China, fried rice is normally prepared from rice left over from the previous day, and it tends to be drier than freshly cooked rice. In my experience, freshly cooked boiled rice can also be used successfully to prepare fried rice, if 10 per cent less water is employed in the original cooking of the rice. Since the rice will be subjected to further cooking during stir-frying, it should end up quite dry and yet well cooked.

A heaped plateful of fried rice eaten in conjunction with a bowlful of soup should be sufficient to appease the hunger of most people with normal appetites. Even those with exceptional appetites should be satisfied with 1½ portions of fried rice, washed down with a portion of soup and a cup or two of tea or another beverage. Here the liquid intake should help to expand the rice and fill up any cavity, real or imagined. One of the presumptions of *Cheap Chow* is that the reader is a person who has a reasonably large appetite. Our portion is, therefore, calculated at 450 gr (1 lb) of solid food, to be washed down with a corresponding amount of soup, together with vegetables and other beverages.

1 Basic fried rice

2 medium onions
4 rashers of bacon
4 eggs
¾ teaspoon salt
3-4 tablespoons vegetable oil
675-900 gr (1½-2 lb) cooked rice
50 gr (2 oz) butter (or margarine)
225 gr (½ lb) green peas (frozen)

Cut onion into thin slices. Slice bacon across lean and fat into thin strips. Beat eggs, adding salt, with a fork for ten seconds.

Heat oil in a large frying pan over medium heat. Add onion and bacon and stir-fry them together for 2½ minutes. Pour in the beaten eggs and allow to flow evenly over the whole pan. When the eggs are about to set, turn and scramble them lightly a few times. Pour in the cooked rice. Spread evenly over the pan to mix, and turn with the egg, bacon and onion. After 1½ minutes remove pan from heat.

Meanwhile, heat butter in a small pan. Add peas and stir them in the butter for three minutes. Pour the peas into the rice, to mix and turn with the other ingredients.

Serve either in a large tureen or salad bowl for the diners to help themselves from, or in individual bowls. *Serves 4-5.*

2 Tomato fried rice

Repeat recipe 1, but add 4-6 firm, medium-size tomatoes. Cut each tomato into quarters or sixths. Add them to heat with the peas, with an extra 1-2 tablespoons of butter, for one extra minute. When cooked, add them together with the peas, and mix and turn with the rice. The addition of the tomatoes will add not only more colour to the dish, but also a distinct freshness of flavour which is very appealing. *Serves 4-5.*

3 Fried rice with carrots and button mushrooms

Repeat recipe 1. In addition use 225 gr (½ lb) young carrots and 225 gr (½ lb) button mushrooms. Dice both carrots and mushrooms fairly small. Use an extra 1-2 tablespoons of butter to fry them for 1½ minutes before adding peas and butter. Fry all together for a further three minutes. When ready add them to the rice and mix all together with the bacon, eggs and onion. A tablespoon or two of soya sauce may be sprinkled over the rice before serving, especially if the diners prefer saltier food. *Serves 4-5.*

4 Fried rice with chopped pork and peas

Repeat recipe 1. In addition use 225 gr (½ lb) of pork (lean, or lean and fat). The pork should be diced into small cubes and then stir-fried quickly in 2 tablespoons of oil for 2½ minutes over high heat. Reduce the heat to low and add 1½ tablespoons soya sauce and ¾ teaspoon of sugar. Continue to stir-fry for one minute, when the pork should be well cooked. The cooked pork is then added to the rice, and tossed and mixed with all the other ingredients. The diced pork, being deep brown in colour and quite salty, should act as a contrast to the other materials and ingredients in the dish. *Serves 4-5.*

5 Fried rice with chopped lamb, beef, kidney, liver, chicken, duck

Any of the above meats or poultry, or a mixture of these, can be used and treated in the same manner as was the pork in the previous recipe then added to, tossed and mixed with the basic fried rice. If no more than 225 gr (½ lb) of meat is used, the initial stir-frying over high heat need not exceed one minute, before the soya sauce (1 tablespoon) and ¾ teaspoon of sugar are added for a further one minute of stir-frying; then the meat or meats are added to mix with the basic fried rice. In the case of chicken or duck, the meat can be just scrapings from the carcase (of boiled or roasted birds, of which, in Western cooking, little use would be made) but try to dice what meats there are into meat cubes, if only to avoid a messy appearance – this is something we have to make an effort to avoid in mixed cooking.

A useful ingredient to add into the stir-frying of meat or poultry at the last moment is a tablespoon or two of chopped spring onions (including all the green parts); this often helps to make the fried rice much more aromatic. *Serves 4-5.*

6 Fried rice with salted fish

Kedgeree is a well-known dish in the British Isles. We Chinese also have our own version of it. The principal difference lies probably in our frying the fish (chopped) before mixing it into the basic fried rice flavoured with other ingredients such as onions, egg and bacon. Salt fish of all types is consumed in quantity in China. It is in our tradition to slow-fry them in oil until they are completely crispy (a process which, incidentally, produces a considerable smell!). Nevertheless, the end product is highly palatable, especially when eaten with rice, and a very small quantity goes a very long way – 25 gr (1 oz) can easily go with 450 gr (1 lb) of cooked rice.

Since smoked fish – such as smoked haddock, kippers, etc. – is widely available in the West, it can be used to produce the Chinese version of fried-rice kedgeree. As the Western smoked fish are not as strong-tasting as the Chinese fried salted fish, somewhat larger quantities are needed and it is necessary to remove as many of the bones as possible (since one of the pleasures of eating fried rice is the tucking-in sensation, which can be spoiled if one has to look and feel for bones all the time). Instead of just poaching the fish, fry it in butter or oil for a couple of minutes after flaking it.

If the fish is found to be not quite salty enough at this stage there would be no harm in adding one tablespoon of soya sauce to fry with it; the sauce should enhance both the colour and flavour of the fish. The appeal of fried-rice kedgeree lies partly in the contrast between the saltiness of the fish and the blandness of rice, and partly in the difference in the texture of the fish to the other ingredients. Because of the dry saltiness of the dish as a whole, it is a dish which should always be accompanied by a bowlful of soup. *Serves 4-5.*

7 Vegetable fried rice

50-75 gr (2-3 oz) braised (salted) Chinese bamboo-shoots (canned)
225 gr (½ lb) bean sprouts
225 gr (½ lb) young carrots
7·5 cm (3 in) section cucumber
100 gr (¼ lb) button mushrooms
2-3 large leaves of cos lettuce
3 tablespoons vegetable oil
2 tablespoons butter
2½ tablespoons soya sauce
1 teaspoon sugar
1·35 kg (3 lb) basic fried rice (less bacon)

Clean vegetables thoroughly and roughly chop them all (except of course bean sprouts, which can be used as they are). Heat oil and butter in a large saucepan. When the butter has melted, add all the vegetables and turn them over high heat for 3 minutes. Add soya sauce and sugar and continue to turn and stir until all vegetables are well lubricated. Add the basic fried rice into the vegetables. Continue to cook and mix over medium heat for 2 minutes.

Vegetable fried rice is best eaten with a selection of pickles and chutneys, and a bowlful of soup to each person. *Serves 4-5.*

Vegetable rice

Vegetable rice differs from fried rice in that the vegetables are cooked in the rice. In fried rice, as we have seen, the chopped or diced ingredients – usually the salty types – are stir-fried into the pre-boiled rice. With vegetable rice, the vegetables are chopped in large pieces and cooked together with the rice from the beginning. Since vegetables usually release some liquid during cooking, the water added to the rice should usually not exceed one-and-a-quarter times the volume of rice used (especially if there is a good quantity of vegetables incorporated). This gives the rice a fresh vegetable flavour, which many people welcome, and which should not be too much compromised by the introduction of too many other extraneous highly-flavoured ingredients; though the addition of a small amount of oil/butter (1-2 tablespoons) is often recommended.

The accompanying savoury dish should be a pure meat dish (such as red-cooked meat), or minced meat, or often in China a 'Tou Fu' (bean-curd) dish cooked with minced meat, and not infrequently with some mushrooms, which provides the vegetable flavour and texture nearest to meat.

1 Spring green (or cabbage) vegetable rice

675 gr (1½ lb) rice
675-900 gr (1½-2 lb) spring greens or cabbage
7·5-9 dl (1¼-1½ pints) water
1 teaspoon salt
1½ tablespoons vegetable oil
1½ tablespoons butter

Rinse rice in two changes of water. Clean and shred greens or cabbage, including stems.

Place rice and vegetable evenly distributed at the bottom of a large heavy pan. Add water, sprinkle contents with salt and bring to boil. Add oil and butter. Stir a few times and close the lid. Reduce heat to very low and insert an asbestos sheet under the pan. Let simmer gently for twelve minutes, then turn heat off and leave contents to cook in their own heat for a further twelve minutes, when the vegetable rice should be ready.

This is a pure vegetable dish. I think it is best eaten with a meat dish – such as red-cooked meat – with a generous amount of gravy. Pickles and chutneys are also good accompaniments. Soups served with vegetable rice should be meat-stock based. *Serves 4-5.*

2 Carrot and courgette vegetable rice

2 tablespoons vegetable oil
1½ tablespoons butter
325 gr (¾ lb) young carrots
325 gr (¾ lb) courgettes
1 teaspoon salt
675 gr (1½ lb) rice
7·5-9 dl (1¼-1½ pints) water

Clean and cut carrots and courgettes diagonally into 2·5-cm (1-in) segments.

Heat oil and butter at the bottom of a large saucepan. Add carrots and stir-fry over high heat for 2½ minutes, add courgettes and salt, and continue to stir-fry together for a further 2 minutes. Add the rice and water. Bring contents to boil. Reduce heat, insert an asbestos sheet under the pan, and leave to simmer gently for 12 minutes. Turn off heat and leave contents to cook in their own heat under firm cover for a further 12 minutes, when the vegetable rice should be well cooked.

This dish of vegetable bulk-food is best eaten with a meat dish or a meat-and-bean-curd dish (bean-curd being an extension of meat) and washed down with a meat-based soup. For vegetarians, a 'hot', salty or savoury vegetable dish should be served with it. Once again pickles and chutneys are useful items to accompany this vegetable rice. *Serves 4-5.*

3 Brussels sprouts (or broccoli) vegetable rice with tomatoes

675 gr (1½ lb) rice
7·5 dl (1¼ pints) water
675 gr (1½ lb) brussels sprouts
4-6 medium tomatoes, quartered
2 tablespoons vegetable oil
1½ tablespoons butter
1½ tablespoons soya sauce

Rinse rice in two changes of water. Drain. Clean sprouts, remove imperfect leaves and cut each sprout into two.

Heat oil and butter in a heavy saucepan. Add sprouts and turn them in the oil and fat for 2 minutes. Add rice and mix it with the sprouts over medium heat for 2 minutes. Pour in the water and bring to boil. Insert an asbestos sheet under the pan and reduce heat. Leave to simmer under cover for 5 minutes. Open the lid and distribute the pieces of tomato evenly over the surface of the rice. Close lid and leave contents to simmer for 6-7 minutes. Turn off heat and leave contents to cook in their own heat for 12 minutes. Open lid, sprinkle contents with soya sauce and serve. *Serves 4-5.*

4 Mixed vegetable 'vegetable rice'

225 gr (½ lb) young carrots
225 gr (½ lb) cauliflower
2 medium sweet peppers
225 gr (½ lb) frozen peas
2 tablespoons vegetable oil
2 tablespoons butter
675 gr (1½ lb) rice
9 dl (1½ pints) water
2 tablespoons soya sauce

Scrape and cut carrots diagonally into 1·25-cm (½-in) segments. Break cauliflower into individual flowerets. Cut peppers into 1·25-cm (½-in) by 3·75-cm (1½-in) slices. Thaw peas.

Heat oil and butter in a heavy pan. Add carrots, cauliflower and peppers. Turn them in the oil for 2 minutes. Add rice and mix and turn them together for 2 minutes over medium heat. Pour in the water and bring to the boil. Insert an asbestos sheet under the pan and leave contents to simmer for 7-8 minutes. Open lid and distribute the peas evenly on the surface of the rice. Close lid and continue to simmer for 5 minutes. Turn heat off and leave contents to cook in their own heat for 12 minutes.

Before serving, open lid and sprinkle contents with soya sauce. *Serves 4-5.*

5 Chinese Buddhists' mixed vegetable rice

2 cakes bean-curd (Tou Fu)
oil for deep frying
325 gr (¾ lb) spring greens
225 gr (½ lb) bamboo shoots
675 gr (1½ lb) rice
2 tablespoons butter
225-325 gr (½-¾ lb) small button mushrooms (or field mushrooms)
9 dl (1½ pints) of water
1½ tablespoons soya sauce

Cut each piece of Tou Fu into 4-6 bits. Deep fry them in oil for 2 minutes. Drain. Cut spring greens into 1·25-cm (½-in) slices. Cut bamboo-shoots into triangular wedges. Rinse rice in two changes of water.

Heat 2 tablespoons of oil and the butter in a heavy saucepan or casserole. Add greens and mushrooms. Turn them over medium heat for 2 minutes. Add the rice and turn in the oil with the other ingredients over medium heat for 2 minutes. Pour in the water. Bring to boil and leave to simmer for 5-6 minutes. Add the bean-curd, then spread the mixture evenly over the rice. Insert an asbestos sheet under the pan, reduce heat to very low and leave contents to simmer under cover for 7-8 minutes. Turn heat off and leave contents to cook in their own heat for 12 minutes.

Before serving, open lid and sprinkle contents with soya sauce. *Serves 4-5.*

6 Summer vegetable rice

100 gr (¼ lb) lotus seeds (optional)	2 tablespoons butter
⅓ of a large cucumber	100 gr (¼ lb) green peas
1 bunch of watercress	675 gr (1½ lb) rice
225 gr (½ lb) lettuce	9 dl (1½ pints) water
2 tablespoons vegetable oil	2 tablespoons soya sauce

Parboil the lotus seeds for 5 minutes and drain (peanuts can be used instead of lotus seeds). Dice cucumber (including skin) into 1·25-cm (½-in) cubes. Wash watercress and remove roots. With scissors, cut each length of watercress into half. Cut lettuce into slices.

Heat oil and butter in a heavy saucepan or casserole. Add all the vegetables and turn them for 2 minutes. Add the rice and turn in the oil with the other ingredients over medium heat for 2 minutes. Pour in the water. Bring to boil and insert an asbestos sheet under the pan. Leave contents to simmer gently under cover for 12 minutes. Turn off the heat and allow the contents to cook in their own heat for another 12 minutes.

Before serving, open lid and sprinkle the contents with soya sauce. *Serves 4-5.*

2 Soups

Soups are, as we have seen, an essential part of a Chinese meal, as we do not normally have water on the table. In the West, Chinese food can be 'watered down' with any long drink, such as beer or a dry, light wine. But for connoisseurs of Chinese food, especially in cold weather, eating hot rice and savoury dishes, together with hot soup, provides a double-heating process that amounts to almost the stoking up of one's central-heating system – which nobody should be denied!

Except for vegetarian dishes, Chinese soups are almost invariably made from a base of bone- or meat-stock, which need not be expensive – even in times of inflation or shortage. The way to make a good basic stock is to simmer the ingredients over a low heat over a long period of time, say 1½-3 hours. Generally 5-6 times the weight of water should be added to the chosen ingredients used. After the initial boiling of 8-10 minutes (when as much as possible of the scum that floats to the top should be skimmed away), the heat should be reduced to its lowest point. Use an asbestos sheet under the pan; or if a casserole is used, place it in an oven at 140°C, 275°F, gas 1. At the end of the cooking time, a chicken stock cube and additional seasoning may be added. When so prepared the stock should become quite meaty and savoury and will make an excellent basis for any type of Chinese soup. A gallon of such basic stock should cost very little indeed and should be available at all times in a well-provisioned Chinese kitchen. For higher-grade and more refined soups, what we usually do in China is add a small amount of fresh meat or vegetables into the pot just a few minutes before the stock is served: this has the effect of imparting greater freshness. To transform such stock into one of the numerous Chinese soups is both quick and easy, as we shall see from the following recipes.

1 Chinese 'egg-flower' soup

2 eggs
2 chicken stock cubes
1·5 litres (2½ pints) of good stock
salt and pepper to taste
2 teaspoons vegetable oil (corn, olive, peanut, sesame)
1 heaped tablespoon chopped spring onions

Beat eggs with fork for 8-10 seconds. Add stock cubes to stock and bring to the boil. Allow them to dissolve. Turn heat to very low. Stream the beaten egg into the stock, very slowly, trailing it evenly over the surface of the soup. Allow egg to set (¼ minute). Stir once. Adjust seasoning to taste.

Place oil and chopped spring onions at the bottom of a large bowl or tureen, or divide into individual bowls, then pour in the soup. *Serves 5-6.*

2 Chinese cabbage soup

This soup is made in two stages: the simmering of the stems of cabbage for one hour and the simmering of cabbage leaves for 15-20 minutes.

1 additional large stem of cabbage (100-200 gr, 4-8 oz)
550 gr (1¼ lb) hard or Savoy cabbage
1 tablespoon lard or butter
1·5 litres (2½ pints) stock
2 chicken stock cubes
salt and pepper to taste

Clean thoroughly and cut additional cabbage stem into a dozen or so neat oblong pieces. Remove stem from the cabbage and cut into similar pieces. Cut cabbage leaves into 2·5-cm (1-in) slices.

Heat lard or butter in a large saucepan or casserole. Add all the cabbage stems. Stir-fry over medium heat for 4-5 minutes.

Pour in the stock and bring to gentle boil. Reduce heat and allow contents to simmer very gently for 1¼ hours, either over very low heat (with asbestos sheet inserted under the pan) or in the oven at 140°C, 275°F, gas 1.

Add stock cubes and cabbage leaves. Bring soup to boil and allow contents to simmer for a further 20 minutes. Season to taste and serve. *Serves 5-6.*

3 Fish-head, onion and watercress soup

Since fish-heads are not often used in cooking in the West, they can usually be obtained for very little, or for free; yet they can be made into delicious soups, much prized in South and Coastal China.

675 gr (1½ lb) fish-heads
2·4 litres (4 pints) water
1½ teaspoons salt
3 slices root ginger
2-3 rashers bacon
2-3 bundles watercress
1½ tablespoons butter or lard
3-4 medium onions, finely sliced
2 chicken stock cubes
pepper to taste
1 tablespoon soya sauce
1 tablespoon vinegar

Clean and rinse fish-heads thoroughly under running water. Place them in a saucepan, add water, salt and ginger and bring to the boil. Simmer very gently (insert an asbestos sheet under the pan) for 1½ hours. Strain through meshed filter and discard bones and heads. Put fish stock aside for later use. Slice bacon, across lean and fat, into shreds. Remove the roots of the watercress and wash thoroughly.

Heat butter or lard in a large saucepan. Add onion and bacon. Sauté them over medium heat for 4 minutes. Stir and turn them over a few times. Pour in the fish stock, bring to the boil and add the stock cubes. Adjust for seasoning (with salt and pepper) and add watercress. Add soya sauce and vinegar. Stir contents around a few times and serve – either in individual bowls or in a large tureen. *Serves 6-8.*

4 Spare-ribs and cucumber soup

As compared with the price of meat, spare-ribs are still reasonably cheap (those spare-ribs sometimes called 'Chinese spare-ribs' are cut from the rib-cage backing on to the 'belly of pork', and are not what the English call spare-ribs).

450 gr (1 lb) spare-ribs	1·2 litres (2 pints) stock
¼-½ medium cucumber	1 chicken stock cube
1 tablespoon lard or butter	salt and pepper to taste
1 medium onion, finely sliced	

Cut spare-ribs into individual ribs. Place them in a saucepan with water. Bring to boil, skim and simmer gently for 1 hour. Cut cucumber into 5-cm (2-in) sections and then slice vertically into double-matchstick strips (including skin).

Heat fat in a saucepan. Add onion and sauté for 2-3 minutes. Add the spare-ribs, and continue to cook over medium heat for 5 minutes. Pour in the stock and add the stock cube. Bring contents to gentle boil and adjust for seasoning with salt and pepper. Add the cucumber. Boil gently for a couple of minutes. Stir the contents around a few times. Serve either in individual bowls (approximately 1-2 ribs per person), or in a large tureen. *Serves 5-6.*

5 Chinese chicken, noodle and spinach soup

450 gr (1 lb) spinach	1½ chicken stock cubes
2·1-2·4 litres (3½-4 pints) meat bone stock	salt, pepper and soya sauce to taste
225 gr (½ lb) egg noodles	2 tablespoons lard or butter
100 gr (¼ lb) cooked chicken meat (or what can be scraped from a chicken carcase)	

Clean spinach thoroughly and cut into slices. Heat stock in a saucepan. Add noodles and simmer gently for 10 minutes. Add shredded chicken and stock cubes and adjust for seasoning with salt, soya sauce and pepper.

Heat lard or butter in a large saucepan. Add spinach and turn it in the hot fat over high heat for 2-3 minutes. Pour in the contents from the first saucepan, and simmer gently for 4-5 minutes. Stir and serve, either in individual bowls or in a large tureen set at the centre of the dining table. *Serves 5-6.*

6 Egg and tomato soup

2 eggs
4-6 medium tomatoes
1·5 litres (2½ pints) good stock
1 chicken stock cube
1 small can tomato soup
salt and pepper to taste
1 tablespoon chopped spring onions (or chives)

Beat eggs with fork for 8-10 seconds. Cut each tomato vertically into 4-6 sections.

Heat stock in a saucepan. Add tomatoes and stock cube and leave to simmer for 5-6 minutes. Add canned tomato soup. Stir until the soup reboils. Turn heat to simmer and adjust for seasoning with salt and pepper. Stream in the beaten egg, trailing it over the surface of the soup. As soon as the egg sets (in ¼ minute) and immediately before serving, sprinkle the chopped spring onion over the surface of the soup. *Serves 5-6.*

7 Sweet corn, chicken and green pea soup

2 tablespoons cornflour
1·5 litres (2½ pints) bone or meat stock
1½-2 medium cans sweet corn
100 gr (¼ lb) cooked chicken meat (or scrapings from carcase)
100 gr (¼ lb) green peas (frozen)
2 chicken stock cubes
salt and pepper to taste
1 tomato, chopped into small pieces

Mix cornflour in 6 dl (1 pint) stock until well blended. Heat remaining stock in a large saucepan. Add sweet corn, chicken and peas. Bring to boil and add stock cubes. Stir and adjust for seasoning with salt and pepper. Pour in the stock/cornflour mixture. Stir over medium heat until the stock thickens.

Sprinkle the top of the soup with chopped tomatoes. The colour contrast of the yellow corn, the green of the peas and the red spots of tomato makes for an attractive appearance. Serve in the usual manner. *Serves 6-7.*

8 Celery, potato, marrow and carrot soup

675 gr (1½ lb) potatoes
325 gr (¾ lb) marrow
325 gr (¾ lb) carrots
325 gr (¾ lb) celery
2 tablespoons lard or butter
2 litres (3¼ pints) bone or meat stock
2 chicken stock cubes

4.5 dl (¾ pint) milk (blended with 1 dessertspoon cornflour)
225 gr (½ lb) green peas (frozen)
salt and pepper to taste

Peel and cut potatoes, marrow and carrots into 1·25 × 2·5 × 2·5-cm (½ × 1 × 1-in) pieces. Cut celery into 1·25-cm (½-in) slices.

Heat lard or butter in a saucepan. Add carrots and stir-fry them over medium heat for 2-3 minutes. Add potatoes and turn them with the carrots until well mixed. Leave to sauté for 5 minutes over medium heat. Pour in the stock, bring to the boil and simmer gently for 25-30 minutes. Add stock cubes, milk, celery, marrow and peas. Bring to boil and simmer gently for 15 minutes. Adjust for seasoning with salt and pepper and turn over contents a few times. Serve either in a very large tureen or in individual bowls. For fewer than 8-10 people, the soup can constitute a meal in itself if each person is served with 1½-2 portions of it. *Serves 8-10.*

9 Hot and sour soup

Hot and sour soup is a traditional Chinese dish of the North. It is usually thick and savoury, with quantities of vinegar and pepper added – a very suitable accompaniment to a winter meal.

225 gr (½ lb) potatoes (or bean-curd if available)
150 gr (6 oz) mushrooms and mushroom stalks (plus 50 gr or 2 oz dried mushrooms if available)
1·5 litres (2½ pints) bone or meat stock
2 chicken stock cubes
¼-½ teaspoon salt and freshly ground pepper
2 tablespoons cornflour
1 tablespoon lard
100 gr (¼ lb) minced meat (or scrapings from a poultry carcase)
50 gr (2 oz) green peas
3 tablespoons soya sauce
3-4 tablespoons vinegar
1 tablespoon sesame oil

Dice potatoes, mushrooms, dried mushrooms – after 20 minutes' soaking in 3 dl (½ pint) water – into 1·25-cm (½-in) cubes. Cook and simmer in 1·2 litres (2 pints) of the stock for ½ hour (add any bits of smoked fish, such as haddock or dried shrimps if available). Add one chicken stock cube and adjust for seasoning with salt. Mix cornflour with 3 dl (½ pint) stock until well blended. Heat lard in a large saucepan. Add minced meat and stir-fry for

3 minutes. Add peas and salt and saute over low heat for 3 minutes. Pour the contents of the first pan into the larger saucepan. Add stock and cornflour mixture, then turn and mix the contents together. Simmer for 10 minutes, then add the second chicken stock cube, soya sauce, mushroom water (left over from soaking the dried mushrooms), vinegar and pepper. Stir and mix them well together. Sprinkle with sesame oil and serve either in a large tureen or in individual bowls. *Serves 5-6.*

10 Broad bean, potato and belly-of-pork soup

325 gr (¾ lb) belly of pork
675 gr (1½ lb) potatoes
1 pair pig's trotters
2 litres (3½ pints) water
450 gr (1 lb) broad beans
2 chicken stock cubes
2 tablespoons soya sauce
salt and pepper to taste
3 tablespoons sherry

Cut pork and potatoes into 2·5-cm (1-in) pieces.

Place trotters and pork in a large casserole. Pour in water to cover and bring to the boil. Reduce heat and simmer gently for 1 hour. Skim away excess fat. Add the broad beans and potatoes. Bring to boil and simmer very gently (insert an asbestos sheet under the casserole, or place in oven at 140°C, 275°F, gas 1) for 1 hour. Add stock cubes and soya sauce. Stir them in with the other contents and adjust for seasoning. Continue to simmer for 10 minutes. Sprinkle with sherry and serve in a very large bowl or tureen for the diners to help themselves from. The soup can be served as a main meal, if each person is served with 1½-2 portions. *Serves 6-8.*

3 Red-cooked meat and fish dishes

There are at least two types of inexpensive meat dishes that can be used as accompaniments to bulk foods. They are the 'red-cooked' meat dishes and the 'stir-fried' meat dishes: the red-cooked dishes are the ones where the meat is slow-braised or slow-simmered in soya sauce, and the stir-fried dishes are the ones where thinly sliced meats or shredded meats are cross-cooked over a high heat with other ingredients – mainly vegetables – which are similarly thinly sliced or shredded.

In Chinese eating, even among the poor, there will usually be some savoury accompaniments on the table to go with the bulk food. These increase in both size and variety as you go up the social and financial scale. When you are amongst the well-to-do and wealthy, there would normally be one or two soups on the table and four or five savoury dishes to accompany rice or (in the North) steamed buns ('Man To'). For the average family, there would be one soup and three or four savoury dishes. Among the poor, there would be just one or two dishes and possibly a soup. The dishes would consist of something quite salty, such as salt fish, or some fatty meat (perhaps 50-100 gr or 2-4 oz) cross-cooked with some vegetables and some pickles, and there would usually be a pure vegetable dish. The soup would consist of some chicken or meat bones (or occasionally the head or claws of chicken, if such extravagances were available) boiled up with some basic vegetables, such as turnips and stems or roots of cabbage and carrots.

The meals in the dining halls of more than half the schools in China during the 1920s and 1930s would normally sink to this level. Although it may not seem very appetizing, this was sufficient to keep one going – although you were likely almost always to feel hungry and be craving for supplementary foods: anything which contained fat, which is savoury (for there was a persistent lack of oil or fat in the system), or anything sweet; and to sink one's teeth into a sizeable piece of meat was to rise to heaven! From the purely nutritional point of view what was missing in the diet was not so much the minerals, vitamins and carbohydrates, but protein (which is occasionally made up by the intake of Tou Fu – or bean-curd cakes). I have a suspicion that it was a lack of the tradition of having milk – and the calcium in milk – during the growing years that caused the average Chinese stature to be smaller than that of the Teutonic and Anglo-Saxon races.

One thing to note about Chinese food preparation is that although some dishes (the stir-fried types) can be labour-intensive, they are usually aimed at a communal meal for four, five or more people. Should there be only two or three people eating (or just one) the correct thing to do is to keep the unused food for another meal or for a series of meals. We always did this in China, even in the past when there was no refrigeration (at a time when even the 'ice box', which was kept cold by using ice buried in the winter and dug up for use in the summer, was rare). We knew, however, that the majority of meat dishes which were cooked in soya sauce – the so-called 'red-cooked' dishes, sometimes also called 'soya-braised' – seemed to keep very well for several days at room temperature, and in some cases even improved with keeping and reheating.

'Reheating' is not a dirty word in Chinese cooking as it is in Western catering. The majority of Chinese in the past died of TB, cholera, plague, typhoid, dysentery, scarlet fever or straightforward undernourishment (slow starvation). I have a suspicion that meat cooked in soya sauce, with some traces of sugar and wine added, is not an ideal breeding ground for bacteria.

On the other hand, cross-cooked, mixed dishes, where meats are cooked with vegetables, are less favourable for keeping for any length of time, and are normally eaten in China almost straight from the pan. When, however, these latter dishes are reheated, a small amount of fresh vegetables, as well as oil and other flavouring ingredients are usually added to bring the dish to life again, when stir-frying it in a frying pan heated to a temperature at least twice that of boiling water for a short period. All these circumstances and treatments are calculated to knock the life out of most harmful bacteria, or at least render them less active. In the West today, where the refrigerator is standard equipment in the kitchen, keeping food for several days is no problem at all. Circumstances, therefore, favour Chinese food preparation, for many Chinese dishes can be cooked in quantity and, if not used or consumed immediately, can be revived at a moment's notice by simply reheating or stir-frying them up with a few spoonfuls of fresh ingredients and materials, to be presented again with pride. Red-cooked dishes can all be revived, when required, by reheating, and the majority of them can be kept in the refrigerator for at least three to four days.

Red-cooked or soya-braised meat dishes

The principal technique used in red-cooking is *low-heat slow cooking* with the minimal addition of water or stock. The only flavouring ingredients added are soya sauce (about 1½-2 tablespoons to 450 gr or 1 lb of meat and bone), perhaps an equivalent amount of wine and 1 teaspoon of sugar. Because of the small liquid content (although a few tablespoons of stock or water may be added) it is essential to see that the heat employed is minimal (after the initial heat-up) so that the food will not burn during the 1½-2½ hours of cooking or even longer. Hence, an asbestos sheet inserted under the pan is useful if the cooking is done on the top of the stove. On the other hand, slow simmering can probably best be done in an oven heated to no more than 140°C, 275°F, gas 1. All red-cooking takes a long time, but since the ingredients need very little preparation, it is, in fact, quite labour saving, as the following recipes should demonstrate. For the purposes of Cheap Chow, all the less expensive cuts of pork or any other type of meat can be successfully used.

1 Red-cooked pork

For this recipe use hand, spring, shank, belly, blade, spare-rib joint or Chinese spare-ribs; do not trim off the skin.

4-5 tablespoons vegetable oil
1·35 kg (3 lb) pork (any one of the above varieties)
4-5 tablespoons soya sauce
6-7 tablespoons red wine or sherry
6-7 tablespoons water
2 teaspoons sugar

Heat oil in a casserole. Add meat in one piece, and turn it over medium heat for 5-6 minutes. Reduce the heat to low and add half the soya sauce, half the wine, half the water and half the sugar. Stir the meat in the 'sauce' a few times, close the lid of the casserole and insert it into an oven pre-heated to 150°C, 300°F, gas 2 for 1 hour, turning the meat every 30 minutes. Add the remainder of the soya sauce, wine, water and sugar and continue to cook in the oven at 140°C, 275°F, gas 1, for a further 1½-1¾ hours, turning the meat over three or four times.

By the time the meat has been cooked for 2½-2¾ hours, the gravy should have become quite thick and sticky and the skin of the pork jelly-like. The meat should be tender enough to be easily sliced from the bone or taken off with a pair of chopsticks. This combination of meat, fat, skin and gravy is probably about the most savoury and appetizing thing in the whole realm of Chinese culinary creation; 2-4 tablespoons of it should be sufficient, eaten with ½-¾ bowl of rice. With plain boiled rice, pork dishes such as this are best eaten with a pure vegetable dish as the second accompaniment. Eaten with congee or rice-gruel, or vegetable rice, no vegetable accompaniment is necessary. If one wishes to be extravagant one can eat 5-6 tablespoons of this pork and gravy with the same amount of boiled rice (½-¾ bowl). It can also accompany all noodle and pasta dishes. *Serves 6-8.*

2 Red-cooked beef (flank, shin, brisket, leg)

Beef is red-cooked in much the same way as pork. Turn meat (in one piece) in hot oil in a casserole for 5-6 minutes. Reduce the heat to low and add half of each of the soya sauce, the wine, the water and the sugar. Stir, close the lid of the casserole and put in a pre-heated oven at 150°C, 300°F, gas 2 for 1 hour, turning the meat twice. Add the remainder of the soya sauce, wine, water and sugar, together with a couple of slices of root ginger and (if available) a couple of pieces of star anise, or two small pieces of dried tangerine peel, or both, or alternatively a bouquet garni, with an extra 4 tablespoons of water. This should add a herbal flavour to the meat, which many find appealing. Continue to cook at 140°C, 275°F, gas 1 for a further 2-2½ hours, turning the meat over occasionally. To the Chinese, beef is a strong-tasting meat, the flavour of which seems to improve or become more acceptable with some herbal flavour incorporated. *Serves 6-8.*

3 Red-cooked lamb or mutton

Lamb or mutton is to the Chinese another strong-tasting meat, and therefore some herbal flavour should be added. As with beef (see recipe 2), add ginger, star anise, dried tangerine peel or bouquet garni. The other flavouring ingredients employed – soya sauce, wine, sugar – should be the same as for pork and beef. Lamb, however, requires less cooking than beef: 1½ hours should be sufficient for lamb, and 2-2¼ hours for mutton. The heat should, as usual, be kept low and steady throughout, after the initial heat-up, and following the addition of the liquid flavouring ingredients. The meat should be turned in the sauce or gravy every 20 minutes; it should be cut into bite-size pieces only after the cooking has been completed, or it can be cut into 3-4 pieces to start with. *Serves 6-8.*

4 Red-cooked chicken

Since the advent of factory-produced 'battery chickens' on to the market, chicken has become one of the cheapest and most widely used forms of poultry meats, hence its suitability for inclusion as material for Cheap Chow dishes. Since most frozen battery-produced chickens have a rankness and 'metallic' flavour about them which is not too appealing, and they also lack the taste of the free-run variety, the red-cooked (or soya-braised) method is undoubtedly one of the best ways to prepare chicken. The use of root ginger, where available, helps to remove these flavours and the addition of soya sauce, sugar and wine imparts the richness of flavour that is often lacking. When red-cooked and smothered in plenty of sauce or thick gravy, battery-produced chickens can become as tasty as the best free-run chickens.

1 chicken, about 1·5 kg (3¼ lb)
4-5 tablespoons vegetable oil
2 slices root ginger
5-6 tablespoons soya sauce
2 teaspoons sugar
7-8 tablespoons stock or water
6-7 tablespoons red wine

Clean chicken thoroughly by dipping it in boiling water and drying carefully. Heat oil in a casserole. When hot, add chicken and brown it in the oil by frying it over high heat, turning frequently, for 5-6 minutes. Drain away excess oil. Add ginger and approximately half of all the other ingredients. Turn the chicken in the mixture for 3-4 minutes over medium heat. Place casserole in oven, pre-heated to 150°C, 300°F, gas 2. Leave to 'pot roast' under cover for 1 hour, turning the bird over four times. Add the balance of soya sauce, sugar, stock or water and wine. Cook at the same temperature for a further 45 minutes, turning the bird over three times in the process.

After 1 hour 45 minutes' cooking, the chicken should be tender enough to take to pieces with a pair of chopsticks and should, therefore, be served on a well-heated, deep-sided dish on the table, for the diners to help themselves from. Alternatively, chicken so cooked can be first chopped up, right through the bones, into large bite-size pieces and cooked in the same manner as when it is cooked whole – but when chopped up the cooking time can be reduced by 15 minutes: after frying to brown it, the bird will only need to be pot-roasted (or soya-braised) for 45 minutes, followed by the addition of the balance of ingredients and a further 45 minutes' cooking in the oven at the same temperature. *Serves 6-8.*

Red-cooked fish

Fish does not reheat well, hence red-cooked fish is aimed at providing savoury food for only one meal. As can be seen from the previous recipes, red-cooking is a universal process of cooking, which can be employed to cook almost any form of food material that is intended to be used as a rich, savoury accompaniment to plain bulk food. In China it is frequently used with as great success for fish as for meat. Although some parts of the fish are inedible – such as head, tail and fins – these parts can be included in the cooking to enhance the flavour and increase the quantity and quality of the gravy, which is very much part and parcel of the appeal of red-cooked dishes.

Because of the inevitable fishiness of fish, however, certain strong vegetables, such as garlic, ginger and onion, are always included with red-cooked fish. These are frequently added to the fat (with fish, lard is often used) to flavour it first before the fish is added. The initial frying should last 1½-2 minutes, then the fish is added and turned in the oil for 2-3 minutes, having previously been rubbed with salt and flour. The liquid flavouring ingredients – soya sauce, wine, stock and sugar – are then poured over.

In slightly more elaborate cases, some sliced or shredded fat pork (or bacon), dried mushrooms and spring onions are spread over the fish. The fish is then subjected to 10-25 minutes of slow braising, which can be done either on the cooker or in the oven by wrapping a large sheet of tinfoil over the top of the roasting pan – in the latter case you can place two rashers of bacon under the fish to prevent sticking. Almost any kind of fish can be cooked in this manner.

5 Red-cooked large fish

1·5-2 kg (3¼-4¼ lb) fish (cod, bream, haddock, etc.)
2 teaspoons salt
2 tablespoons flour
3 slices root ginger
3 tablespoons vegetable oil
2 medium onions, finely sliced
2 tablespoons lard
4-5 tablespoons soya sauce
4-5 tablespoons water
4-5 tablespoons red wine (or dry sherry)
2 teaspoons sugar
2-3 stalks spring onion

Clean the fish thoroughly both inside and out. Chop off the head and tail and cut the fish into 5-cm (2-in) oblong pieces. Rub these with salt and flour. Cut ginger into thin shreds.

Heat oil in a large frying pan (with lid) or casserole. Add onion and ginger, fish-head and tail. Turn the contents over a high heat for 3-4 minutes. Push ingredients to one side of pan and add the lard. When it has melted add the pieces of fish and spread them evenly over the pan. Turn the heat low and fry them for 2 minutes on either side. Pour in the soya sauce, water and wine and sprinkle the fish with sugar. Turn the pieces of fish in the mixed sauce until every piece is well covered. Spread spring onion on top of the pieces of fish. Leave to simmer or braise under cover for 8-10 minutes (insert an asbestos sheet under the pan), turning the contents over once.

Remove the fish on to a well-heated dish with the aid of a fish-slice. Pile the spring onion and shredded ginger and onion on top of the fish and pour the gravy over it. Serve with any bulk food (including noodles). *Serves 6-8.*

6 Red-cooked small fish

With small fish like herrings, sprats, etc. the heads, tails and bones can all be eaten if the frying is prolonged enough to crisp the bones. In doing so an extra 3-4 tablespoons of oil should be used and drained away afterwards. The braising, too, should also be lengthened by 5 minutes or so, with the purpose of making the bones more edible, followed by 10 minutes' roasting (or steaming). The spring onion should be sprinkled over the fish only 2-3 minutes before dishing out. When serving, the onion, shredded ginger and spring onion should be piled on top of the piled-up fish, with gravy poured over all. *Serves 6-8.*

The above series of six red-cooked dishes can be made less expensive to prepare by combining the meat or fish with quantities of vegetables – usually the hard or semi-hard type, such as turnips, carrots, cabbage, potatoes, marrow, courgettes, cauliflower, aubergines, etc.; and in the case of fish, with plenty of spring onions, leeks, watercress, tomatoes, etc.

Where meat is combined with vegetables, the meat is usually cut into the size and shape (where possible) of the cut-up vegetables, i.e. in about 2·5-cm (1-in) pieces; and the vegetables are added only after the meat has been cooking for approximately ½ hour. Since vegetables are usually quite cheap when in season, by cooking the same or 1½ times the amount of vegetables as meat, the cost of the dish can frequently be reduced by half, compared with pure meat dishes. Since in *Cheap Chow* we confine ourselves mainly to cheap cuts of meat, the dishes produced should become inexpensive indeed.

But before embarking upon our recipes for mixed meat (or fish) and vegetable dishes, there is an excellent dish that can be prepared from the most common vegetable of all: cabbage. This vegetable, when red-cooked, can often have such succulence and meaty appeal that it can take the place of meat as an accompaniment to bulk foods.

7 Red-cooked cabbage

White, Savoy or spring cabbage can be used for this dish.

1 cabbage, about 1·35 kg (3 lb)
1 chicken stock cube
3 tablespoons vegetable oil
1 medium onion, finely sliced
2 cloves garlic, crushed
4-5 tablespoons water
2 tablespoons butter
4-5 tablespoons soya sauce
2 teaspoons sugar
2-3 tablespoons wine or sherry (optional)
pepper to taste

Clean cabbage and remove any discoloured outer leaves. Carve out the stem and cut it into 2·5-cm (1-in) pieces. Cut cabbage leaves into 2·5-cm (1-in) slices. Crumble stock cube.

Heat oil in a large saucepan. Add onion, garlic and cabbage stems. Stir them in the oil over medium heat for 2 minutes and leave to sauté for 2-3 more minutes. Sprinkle contents with crumbled stock cube and add water. Stir and leave to cook over low heat for 3 minutes. Add butter and all the cabbage. Turn the cabbage over a few times until every leaf is well lubricated with oil and butter.

Add the soya sauce, sugar, wine and pepper to taste. Turn the vegetable around until every piece is well covered with sauce. Reduce heat to low, insert an asbestos sheet under the pan, and leave to cook for 18-20 minutes. Turn the cabbage over once more during the process of cooking.

Serve in a large, well-heated bowl or deep-sided heatproof dish, as an accompaniment to any plain bulk food – especially with rice dishes. *Serves 5-6.*

8 Red-cooked pork with vegetables

(a) with carrots and turnips (long-cooking)

Refer to recipe 1 of this chapter. Do not vary the quantity of oil (fat) or the flavouring ingredients (soya sauce, stock cube, sugar and wine) used, except the basic main material of the dish, which is pork. Reduce pork by 40-50 per cent, and cook in the same manner for the first hour.

Use about 1½ times the weight of carrots or turnips (or both) as pork. Add them (they should be cut diagonally into 2·5-cm (1-in) pieces) with the balance of the flavouring ingredients. Turn the carrots or turnips in the sauce a few times and leave to cook for a further hour, turning the contents over a couple of times in the process. *Serves 6-8.*

(b) with potato, cabbage, marrow, sprouts, courgettes (medium-cooking)

Refer to the previous recipe. Chop the vegetable (or vegetables) into 2·5-cm (1-in) pieces and add to the pan after the meat has been cooking for 1¼ hours. Stir them in with the pork and gravy. Add the balance of flavouring ingredients. Turn the contents over a few more times and leave them to simmer over low heat for a further 30-35 minutes.

(c) with celery, spinach, mushrooms, peas, tomato, etc. (short-cooking)

Chop the vegetables into about 2·5-cm (1-in) pieces (in the case of mushrooms remove the stalks and add these to the pan containing the meat). Repeat recipe 8a, but add the bulk of the vegetables and balance of flavouring ingredients only 15 minutes before serving. Turn the contents over a couple of times during the last stages of the cooking, which should be over a low heat. *Serves 6-8.*

9 Red-cooked beef with vegetables

(a) with turnips, carrots (long-cooking)

Repeat recipe 2 of this chapter, but reduce the quantity of beef by 40 per cent and use the same weight of vegetables as beef or half as much again (either singly or mixed). The vegetables should be cut diagonally into approximately 2·5-cm (1-in) wedges and added to the pan or casserole after the beef has had its first hour of slow simmering, together with the balance of flavouring ingredients (soya sauce, wine, sugar, star anise, dried tangerine peel or bouquet garni). Because of the quantity of vegetables added into the cooking, an additional 1-1½ tablespoons of beef fat or lard can be added. The contents should be turned over at least 3-4 times during the last 45 minutes of cooking time. *Serves 6-8.*

(b) with cabbage, sprouts, courgettes, marrow, potatoes (medium-cooking)

Repeat recipe 2 of this chapter, but reduce the beef by about 40 per cent and use the same weight of vegetable (or vegetables) as beef, or half as much again. With cabbage and leeks, cut into 2·5-cm (1-in) slices; if onion is used it should be cut into thin slices. With beef, perhaps a little more pepper should be sprinkled over the contents than with pork. The beef should be cooked for 1½ hours, before the vegetables are added; thereafter, continue to cook for 30 minutes more at the same low heat, turning the contents over at least three times in the process. *Serves 6-8.*

(c) with celery, spinach, watercress, tomatoes (short-cooking)

As the vegetables only require very short cooking, they should be added into the pan for the last 10-15 minutes of the cooking, together with the balance of flavouring ingredients, after the beef has been cooking for a full 2 hours over low heat, as in recipe 2. In the case of watercress and spinach, no more weight of these than beef should be used; as for tomatoes and celery, their weight should not be more than 1½ times that of the beef

In the latter case, an extra 1½ teaspoons of beef fat or lard can be added to advantage. The contents should, as usual, be turned over three times during the last stages of their cooking. *Serves 6-8.*

10 Red-cooked lamb or mutton with vegetables

Refer to recipe 3 of this chapter, but reduce the quantity of lamb by about 40 per cent. Since lamb and mutton are bracketed in Chinese cooking with beef as strong-tasting meats, the same vegetables can be used: turnips and carrots for long cooking; cabbage, sprouts, courgettes, marrow, potatoes for medium-length cooking; and celery, spinach, watercress, tomatoes for short cooking.

The long-cooked vegetables should be added to the beef in the pan or casserole for the last hour of cooking; the medium-cooked vegetables should be added for only the last half-hour of cooking; and the short-cooked vegetables need only be incorporated into the pan during the last 5-10 minutes of the cooking. As to the quantity of the vegetables used, these can be of the same weight as the meat, or half as much again. In the case of the latter, an extra 1-1½ tablespoons of butter or lard can be incorporated, to make the vegetables smoother and more succulent. *Serves 6-8.*

11 Red-cooked chicken with vegetables

Repeat recipe 4 of this chapter. When the chicken is cooked with vegetables it is best chopped into 2·5-cm (1-in) pieces. When chopped, the cooking time can be reduced from 1¾ hours to 1½ hours. The vegetables need only be added during the second 45 minutes of the cooking, together with the balance of flavouring ingredients. The best vegetables to use with chicken for this medium-length cooking are potatoes, broad beans, broccoli, courgettes, mushrooms, etc. About the same weight of vegetables as chicken should be cooked together. In this case, perhaps an extra tablespoon or two of soya sauce might be added. One great advantage of such a dish is that most of the chicken's greasiness is absorbed by the vegetables, which then become much smoother and more succulent. *Serves 6-8.*

12 Red-cooked fish with vegetables

Refer to recipes 5 and 6 of this chapter. We have already noted that in Chinese cooking a couple of slices of root ginger are always used in the initial frying to do away with some of the fishy flavour, which, although undoubtedly appealing to cats, does not normally suit the palate of man. If root ginger is not available (being still very inexpensive, it should one day become much more widely used in Western cooking) a small amount of garlic, a reasonable amount of onion or spring onion, and a sprinkling of chopped orange or lemon peel can be used.

After adding the fish to the oil (flavoured with onion, garlic, ginger) the ingredients can all be pushed to one side of the pan or casserole after the initial cooking and the fresh vegetables added, to be fried on the other side, in the oil already in the pan. These vegetables can be of the medium-to-quick-cooking variety, especially the stronger-tasting types, such as spring onions, leeks, celery, mushrooms, tomatoes or shredded turnips and carrots. A smaller amount of the pickled and dried vegetables, such as shredded gherkins, chopped mixed pickles, dried mushrooms (which will need to be soaked in water for 20 minutes) can also be added. Only about one-quarter or less of these dried, salted or pickled vegetables should be used in conjunction with the fresh vegetables, which should be used in a quantity about equal to or somewhat more in weight than the weight of fish employed. Since most of these vegetables would require no more than 4-5 minutes of stir-frying, they should be added into the pan during the last phase of the cooking. Indeed, one of the best ways of producing these fish and vegetable dishes is to pile the cooked fish in the middle of a deep-sided heatproof dish and to surround it with the lightly stir-fried fresh vegetables; then insert the whole dish into a steamer and subject all the contents to 8-10 minutes of vigorous steaming.

So, with such a dish, you may start with no more than 1 kg (2¼ lb) of fish but end up with a dish of savoury foods weighing 2·5 kg (5½ lb), which, when eaten with bulk foods, should be sufficient to satisfy the hunger of no less than *seven, eight, or more people.*

4 Lu – cooking in master sauce

The only time we Chinese indulge in using a fair quantity and variety of herbs and spices is when cooking in 'master sauce', which we call Lu, or Lu T'ang.

It is sufficient to say that since the making of master sauce involves the use of ginger, garlic, onion, sugar and wine, a small amount of the sauce should be adequate – unless one wishes to make the herbal flavour particularly pronounced, or cause one particular herbal flavour to stand out. In China, we sometimes use the 'five-spice powder', which is a mixture of all the various herbs and spices in a dried and powdered form.

Master sauce is therefore a strong and highly savoury herbal sauce (due to the meats and bones cooked in it), which is able to counteract or eliminate any unwanted flavour or smell that is inherent in foods that are in the main appealing but carry with them some blemishes in taste that are best eliminated. All kinds of foods can be cooked in the master sauce, for varying lengths of time, including hard-boiled eggs (which require no more than 10-15 minutes' cooking); but it is most often used to cook the stronger meats: mutton, beef, venison, etc. – and, these days, battery-produced chicken – and, above all, the offal of animals.

When the master sauce has been used for some time, and quantities of meat of one sort or another have been cooked in it, it usually attains a high degree of taste and savouriness. Such sauces are often used to cook food materials which are not in themselves inherently tasty and require savour to be imparted to them: these include bean-curd cakes, dumplings and the hard vegetables. Since in poverty-stricken countries, such as China was in the past, all edible materials have to be pressed into use, master sauce is employed in the kitchen with regularity.

The usual practice in Lu or master sauce cooking is to use large chunks of meat (or vegetables) whole, and then to cut them into neat slices just before serving. This has the advantage of not oversalting (for the standard soya-herbal master sauce is quite salty) or spicing the meat – which would happen if the ingredients or materials were initially cut up and immersed in the sauce.

The dish should consist of neatly cut slices, with the thin outer edge brown, salty and spiced, while the inner parts of the meat (or vegetable) should be fresh and plain-cooked. Such meats cooked in soya-herbal sauce should bear very little resemblance to what the items originally were. Indeed, few Westerners would know what they were eating – except for choice bits and pieces of meaty morsels! These are quite ideal for consumption with practically all forms of bulk foods, especially those where the vegetable elements are already incorporated. Another great advantage of foods cooked in Lu or master sauce is that they can normally be kept for a long time. The strong soya-herbal elements in the sauce seem to have a preservative effect and the meat can often keep a week in the refrigerator, or 2-3 days at room temperature without deteriorating.

Basic master sauce (or Lu T'ang)

The following recipe will make 1·5 litres (2½ pints) of master sauce.

$1\frac{1}{2}$ dl ($\frac{1}{4}$ pint) soya sauce
6 dl (1 pint) wine (red or white)
6 dl (1 pint) bone broth
$1\frac{1}{2}$ dl ($\frac{1}{4}$ pint) water
4-5 slices root ginger
3-4 cloves of garlic
3 medium onions
2-3 envelopes bouquet garni
2-3 tablespoons brown sugar
450 gr-1 kg (1-$2\frac{1}{4}$ lb) cheap cut of beef (leg, shin, flank) or cheap cut of pork (hand, spring or spare-ribs)

Bring the above materials and ingredients to boil in a heavy saucepan, and simmer over low heat (insert an asbestos sheet under the pan) for $1\frac{3}{4}$-2 hours. Remove the meat and cut it into neat slices, for consumption with bulk foods. Strain away the bones and other extraneous matter. The sauce requires other meats to be cooked in it; herbal ingredients should be replenished every 4-5 days in the winter and 2-3 days in the summer, to keep sauce 'alive'.

1 Tripe cooked in master sauce

1 kg ($2\frac{1}{4}$ lb) pork or beef tripe
1·5 litres ($2\frac{1}{2}$ pints) master sauce

Clean the tripe by plunging it into a large pan of boiling water for 3-4 minutes, then rinsing under cold running water.

Bring sauce to boil in a saucepan. Add the tripe and allow it to simmer very gently in the sauce for 1-$1\frac{3}{4}$ hours. Remove tripe to drain. Keep sauce for further use.

When the tripe is cold, cut it into thin slices or shreds and serve with hot boiled rice, rice-gruel (congee) or vegetable rice. Vinegar can be used as a dip for tripe. Alternatively, tripe so cooked can be used to stir-fry together with shredded vegetables in a stir-fried dish, where tripe can be just one of several ingredients. *Serves 6.*

2 Liver and kidney cooked in master sauce

Liver and kidney, being offal, do not need such lengthy cooking as tripe. The cooking time required is partly dependent upon the size of the pieces; normally they should not need to be cooked for more than 15-20 minutes. But for the purpose of flavouring, they may be left to cook in the sauce for a further $\frac{1}{2}$-1 hour.

1 kg (2¼ lb) liver, kidney (lamb, pork or beef)
1·5 litres (2½ pints) master sauce

Remove membranes from kidney and cut each piece in half. If liver weighs more than 325 gr (¾ lb), slice into two pieces. Clean by rinsing under running water.

Bring sauce to boil and add liver and kidney. When sauce reboils, reduce heat to low and simmer very gently for 10-15 minutes. Turn heat off and leave liver and kidney to cook and cool in the lessening heat for 30 minutes. Remove from sauce to drain and cool further.

When cold, cut into neat, thin slices. Arrange these on a serving dish, keeping liver and kidney to different sides of the dish. Serve with hot bulk foods. Can be eaten hot or cold. *Serves 6.*

3 Shin, leg or flank of beef, or cow-heel, cooked in master sauce

The only difference between the methods of cooking these cheap cuts of beef, and those used in the previous recipes, is simply that the cooking must be much longer: usually 2½-3½ hours, but it has to be done over a very low heat if the meat is not to become dry and fibrous. Because of the long cooking, during which a good deal of the sauce can evaporate, an additional 7·5 dl (1¼ pints) of water should be added to the sauce at the beginning.

1 kg (2¼ lb) beef (shin, leg, flank or neck)
1·5 litres (2½ pints) master sauce
7·5 dl (1¼ pints) water

Add water to master sauce and bring to the boil. Add meat – in large pieces – and when the contents reboil, reduce heat to very low (insert an asbestos sheet under the pan); if cooked in a casserole, place in an oven heated to 140°C, 275°F, gas 1. Leave to simmer for 2½-3½ hours. Remove beef from the pan and place on rack or plate to dry.

When meat is quite cool or cold, cut into neat, thin slices. Serve with any hot bulk food, together with plain cooked vegetables. *Serves 6.*

4 Pork (hand, spring, shank or blade) cooked in master sauce

1 kg ($2\frac{1}{4}$ lb) pork (hand, spring, shank or blade)
1·5 litres ($2\frac{1}{2}$ pints) master sauce
3 dl ($\frac{1}{2}$ pint) water

Add water to master sauce and bring to the boil. Add meat. When contents reboil, reduce heat to minimum and insert an asbestos sheet under the pan. Leave to simmer gently for $1\frac{1}{2}$-$1\frac{3}{4}$ hours. Remove pork from sauce and place on rack or plate to drain.

When meat is cold, cut meat and skin from bone in neat pieces (preferably each piece should contain a blend of skin, fat and lean) to be served with any bulk food and vegetables. When a sufficient amount of meat, bone and skin (after first lot of cooking) has been cooked in the sauce, it will jellify when cold. Cool 1·5 dl ($\frac{1}{4}$ pint) of the used sauce in a dish or sauce-boat (in the refrigerator) and use it to supplement meat eaten with bulk foods. *Serves 6.*

5 Spare-ribs cooked in master sauce

1·35 kg (3 lb) Chinese spare-ribs (the rib-cage of belly)
1·5 litres ($2\frac{1}{2}$ pints) master sauce
6 dl (1 pint) water

Dip spare-ribs in large pan of boiling water and parboil for 4-5 minutes. Drain and rinse under cold running water.

Add water to master sauce. Bring to boil and add spare-ribs. When contents reboil, leave to simmer gently for 45-50 minutes over very low heat. Remove ribs from sauce, to drain. When drained and cool, cut into individual ribs and place on rack or roasting pan and insert into pre-heated oven to 200°C, 400°F, gas 6 for 10-12 minutes.

This dish can be served as an appetizer. If used as an accompaniment to bulk foods, it is best to add a similar weight of vegetables that have been chopped to a reasonably large size – approximately 2 × 5 cm (1 × 2 in) – and a further 3 dl ($\frac{1}{2}$ pint) of master sauce. Simmer together for the last 20 minutes and serve as spare-ribs with vegetables. Almost any vegetable can be cooked with spare-ribs: notably cabbage, marrow, broccoli, sprouts, cauliflower, celery, aubergines, onions, carrots, potatoes, mushrooms. *Serves 6.*

6 Vegetables cooked in master sauce

The majority of hard and semi-hard vegetables can be cooked in master sauce and deep-fried for 1-2 minutes before serving.

(a) Carrots, turnips, swedes, potatoes, parsnips, butter beans

The first five vegetables should be cut into pieces (approximately 3·75 cm or 1½ in square) and simmered in the master sauce for 20-25 minutes. They should then be drained. When dry, place in a wire basket and immerse in boiling oil or fat, to fry for 1-2 minutes.

They can then either be drained and served with bulk foods, or further cooked by stir-frying to mix with other plain-cooked foods to form a larger dish, either all-vegetable or a mixture of thinly sliced or shredded meat with vegetables.

(b) Cabbage, cauliflower, broccoli, sprouts, aubergines, green beans, marrow, mushrooms, celery

This second series of semi-hard vegetables can be cooked in master sauce in the same way after being chopped into 2·5 - 3·75-cm (1 - 1½-in) slices (or broken into individual florets in the case of cauliflower and broccoli). (Mushroom stalks should be removed and cooked for an extra 20 minutes.) The vegetables should then be immersed in the master sauce to simmer for 10 minutes. After draining, they should be deep-fried for 2 minutes. When so cooked the vegetables should become highly savoury and can be served with any kind of bulk food. Or, as with the previous series of hard vegetables, they can be further stir-fried with plain-cooked vegetables or meats to form larger all-vegetable or mix-cooked dishes.

Note: After using a master sauce to cook vegetables, it should be renewed by cooking meat or poultry in it before using it again for cooking vegetables.

7 Eggs cooked in master sauce

Eggs are usually hard-boiled first, shelled, and then simmered for 10-15 minutes in the sauce. Drain them and slice into 6-8 segments. By this time the surface of the eggs will have become a rich brown, and the contrast between the whites and yolks is attractive. They are usually served in China with rice-gruel for breakfast or supper, but can be eaten with boiled or vegetable rice.

8 Fish cooked in master sauce

There are occasions in the West when there is a sudden glut of fish, because Westerners are not used to cooking and eating certain types of fish – which may in fact be highly palatable – such as pike, porgy, bluefish, catfish, carp, flounder, mackerel, mullet, perch, smelts, red snapper, yellow pike, eels, etc. These and many others can all be cooked in master sauce.

When one is cooking fish or game the master sauce usually contains more herbs than for cooking meat: simply add a couple of extra packets of bouquet garni and leave to simmer in the master sauce for 10-20 minutes before using. Fish does not usually require prolonged cooking; simply simmer in the master sauce for 4-5 minutes, turn off the heat, and leave to cool and cook in the remaining heat for a further 15 minutes. Then lift out to drain.

Fish can either be deep fried for 3-4 minutes and served covered with quick-fried vegetables, or it can be covered with shredded vegetables (ginger, spring onions, leeks, etc.) and steamed, with a vigorous blast of steam, for 7-8 minutes. Or it can be baked in an oven, covered in tinfoil, for 10-11 minutes at 200°C, 400°F, gas 6. Alternatively, the fish can be laid out on a couple of rashers of bacon in a large frying pan, covered with a pile of shredded vegetables (leeks, spring onions, ginger, watercress, etc.) and 3 dl (½ pint) of the master sauce poured over. Bring the contents to the boil and braise (i.e. baste the fish with the boiling sauce in the pan) for 4-5 minutes. Serve by transferring the fish and sauce to a well-heated dish. Fish cooked first in master sauce, then fried, steamed or braised with additional vegetables is as delicious an accompaniment to bulk food as any meat dish.

(a) Large fish

325 gr (¾ lb) spring onions or leeks (or mixed with shredded celery, mushrooms, tomatoes, watercress, etc.)
2-3 packets bouquet garni
2 litres (3 pints) master sauce
1 kg (2¼ lb) white fish
4-6 tablespoons lard or margarine

Cut spring onions or leeks into 3-cm (1½-in) segments (or shred other vegetables to similar size and length). Add bouquet garni to sauce, simmer gently for 15 minutes and remove. Clean and scrub the fish thoroughly – gut and descale where necessary – and rinse thoroughly in running water. Dry and chop fish into pieces, if too large for pan containing sauce.

Heat sauce in large saucepan or casserole. Add fish, bring to boil and simmer for 4-5 minutes. Turn heat off and leave fish to cook for 15 minutes, turning the fish over a few times. Remove fish from pan, drain thoroughly. Heat lard or margarine in a large frying pan. Place the fish in the fat, and fry over medium heat for 2-3 minutes on either side. Sprinkle spring onion (or any other shredded vegetables) over the fish. Ladle 5-6 tablespoons of master sauce over the fish and vegetables. Leave contents to braise over low heat for a further 4-5 minutes, basting them now and then with the boiling sauce.

Serve the fish in a deep-sided, well-heated oval dish, using the vegetables to dress the fish. Pour over the sauce from the bottom of the pan. *Serves 6-8.*

(b) Small fish (sprats, sardines, herrings, smelts, gudgeons, etc.)

Paradoxically, in Chinese cooking small fish are usually subjected to longer cooking than large fish so that their bones become crisper and more edible. The bones and heads are usually deep-fried, which involves the use of a large quantity of oil. In a modern kitchen they can be grilled or baked.

1 kg (2¼ lb) small fish
3 teaspoons salt
3 tablespoons vinegar
4 tablespoons flour
4 stalks spring onion
3 cloves garlic
2 packets bouquet garni
2 litres (3 pints) master sauce
3 dl (½ pint) vegetable oil
3 tablespoons lard or margarine
4 tablespoons wine (red or white)

Rinse and dry fish thoroughly. Sprinkle and rub with salt and vinegar (especially inside cavity). Turn fish several times and leave to season overnight in the refrigerator. Drain fish, rinse quickly under running water and dry. Dust with flour. Cut spring onion into 2·5-cm (1-in) pieces. Crush garlic. Simmer bouquet garni in master sauce for 20 minutes and remove.

Heat oil in a very large frying pan. When hot, spread the fish over the pan, and fry over high heat for 4 minutes on each side. Drain away as much of the oil as possible. Heat master sauce in a large saucepan. Place all the fish in a wire basket and sink into the master sauce to simmer for 15 minutes. Drain the fish and spread them evenly over the bottom of a roasting pan in which the lard or margarine has been melted. Sprinkle with garlic, spring onion and wine. Heat for 2 minutes on top of the cooker before putting pan into a pre-heated oven at 200°C, 400°F, gas 6. Leave the fish to bake for 20 minutes, by which time they should be quite dry and crisp.

Serve the fish on a well-heated dish and eat with bulk foods, accompanied with a soup. *Serves 6-8.*

5 Curry and minced meat dishes

Curry

In Indian cooking, curry is usually made from numerous spices, herbs, seeds and roots, such as garlic, chillies, coriander, cumin seeds, turmeric, cardamom, cinnamon, cloves, coconut, bay leaf, nutmeg, mustard seed, mango, poppy seed, peppercorn, sesame seed, tamarind, etc. For discriminating cooks the curry powder should be freshly made each day. For our purpose – producing basic but appetizing food that is economical in time and money – we shall simply employ curry powder or curry paste.

Over the centuries, the Chinese have found it easy to accept cooking methods and ingredients that have originated in other countries and cultures. This liberal attitude is probably attributable to the size and range of the Chinese culinary repertoire, into which almost anything can be adapted and absorbed. When curry first appeared on the horizon, it seemed very alien to the Chinese palate, but has now become almost part and parcel of the Chinese cuisine. One reason for this is that curry seems to fall in line with the theory of 'expanding savouriness', whereby a small amount of expensive food can be cooked with curry, then cooked with 2-3 times its own weight of vegetables, to be eaten with a vast amount of bulk food. Thus, curried dishes make a useful contribution to Cheap Chow.

Practically all red-cooked dishes can be curried with splendid results. However, it is more in the curry tradition to have the meat cut into bite-size pieces rather than leaving it in big chunks, bones and all, as we often do in Chinese meat cookery. As with soya sauce, both meat and fish can be curried with equal success. Most vegetables can also be curried, if what is required is not the fresh native taste of vegetables, but something highly flavoursome that will help to accompany bulk food. Indeed, most Chinese dishes that are stir-fried and braised can be made into curried dishes by simply adding curry powder during the early stages of the frying. One type of ingredient that is often added to curried dishes, especially during the period of braising and stewing, is milk, seldom employed in Chinese cookery.

Let us go over a few basic curried dishes, all of which can be used as excellent accompaniments to bulk foods. In all these dishes vegetables are included, which will enlarge the bulk.

1 Curried pork with vegetables

1 kg (2¼ lb) pork (belly, shank, middle-cut or spare-ribs)
3 slices root ginger (if available)
1 kg (2¼ lb) marrow
4 tablespoons vegetable oil or margarine
3 garlic cloves, crushed
2 large onions, finely sliced
1½-2 tablespoons curry powder
3 teaspoons salt
3 dl (½ pint) milk

Cut meat into large bite-size pieces. Crush ginger into small shreds. Remove skin from marrow and cut into cubes about twice the size of the pieces of meat.

Heat oil or margarine in a large heavy saucepan or casserole. Add garlic, ginger, onion and curry powder. Stir-fry for 2 minutes and leave to cook over a gentle heat for 2 minutes. Raise heat to high, add pork, sprinkle with salt. Stir with onion curry. When thoroughly mixed leave to cook over low heat for 30 minutes. Add the pieces of marrow, pour in the milk, adjust for seasoning (salt). Bring contents to boil, turn a few times and place the pan or casserole in a pre-heated oven at 150 C, 300°F, gas 2 for the next 40 minutes, when the pork with vegetables, now weighing at least 2·5 kg (5½ lb) should be ready to serve – with at least the same weight of bulk food. *Serves 8-10.*

2 Curried beef with vegetables

Beef can be treated in exactly the same way as pork, except that it will require nearly twice the length of cooking at a low heat, to tenderize. This can be done by stewing the beef for 40 minutes before the vegetables are added.

1 kg (2¼ lb) beef (flank, shin, brisket or leg)
3 slices ginger
225 gr (½ lb) carrots
1 kg (2¼ lb) potatoes
3-4 tablespoons vegetable oil or margarine
3 cloves garlic, crushed
3 large onions, finely sliced
1½-2 tablespoons curry powder or paste
3-4 teaspoons salt
3 dl (½ pint) bone stock
3 dl (½ pint) milk
675 gr (¾ lb) green peas

Cut meat into large bite-size pieces. Crush ginger into small grains. Scrape and cut carrots diagonally into 2·5-cm (1-in) pieces. Peel potatoes and cut into pieces double the size of the meat.

Heat oil in a large, heavy saucepan or casserole. Add ginger, garlic, onion and curry. Stir-fry them together for 1 minute. Add meat and sprinkle contents with salt. Turn the contents over medium heat for 4-5 minutes. Add stock and carrots. Bring contents to a gentle boil and leave to cook over low heat for 15 minutes. Turn contents over a few times and insert container into a pre-heated oven at 170°C, 325°F, gas 3, to cook for 1 hour.

Place the casserole on top of the cooker. Add potatoes, milk and peas. Turn and mix the contents and adjust seasoning with salt. Leave to simmer over very low heat (insert asbestos sheet under the pan) for 30 minutes, when ready to serve.

The dish should now weigh about 3 kg (6¾ lb), and should be served with at least its own weight of bulk food. *Serves 8-10.*

3 Curried lamb (mutton) with vegetables

To the Chinese, lamb or mutton are stong-tasting meats, like beef; their cooking time should be about half an hour shorter.

1 kg (2¼ lb) lamb (or mutton)
3 slices root ginger
550 gr (1¼ lb) cauliflower
325 gr (¾ lb) green peas
3-4 tablespoons vegetable oil or margarine (or lard)
3 garlic cloves, crushed
2 large onions, finely sliced
1½-2 tablespoons curry powder
3 teaspoons salt
3 dl (½ pint) meat stock
325 gr (¾ lb) leeks, cut into 2·5-cm (1-in) pieces
1 chicken stock cube
3 dl (½ pint) milk

Cut meat into large bite-size pieces. Crush ginger into small shreds. Break cauliflower into individual florets. Thaw peas if frozen.

Heat oil or fat in a large saucepan or casserole. Add ginger, garlic, onion and curry powder. Stir-fry for 1 minute. Add meat and salt and continue to turn and stir-fry for 2-3 minutes. Then leave to cook over low/medium heat for 15 minutes. Add stock, mix contents together and insert casserole into a pre-heated oven set at 170°C, 325°F, gas 3 for 1 hour.

Place casserole on top of cooker. Add leeks, cauliflower, peas, stock cube and milk. Adjust for seasoning with salt. Leave to cook for 15 minutes, then serve, with at least its own weight of rice. *Serves 8-10.*

4 Curried chicken with vegetables

1 kg (2¼ lb) chicken
3 slices root ginger
2 medium green or red sweet peppers
1 medium cauliflower
1 kg (2¼ lb) potatoes
4 tablespoons oil or fat
2 large onions, finely sliced
3 garlic cloves, crushed
1½-2 tablespoons curry powder
3 teaspoons salt
3 dl (½ pint) meat or bone stock
2 chicken stock cubes
3 dl (½ pint) milk

Clean and chop chicken through bone into large bite-size pieces. Cut its liver and kidneys into three pieces each. Crush ginger into small grains. Cut peppers into 2·5-cm (1-in) strips. Break cauliflower into individual branchlets. Peel and cut potatoes into thin wedges.

Heat oil or fat in a large saucepan or casserole. Add onion, garlic, ginger and curry powder. Stir-fry together over medium heat for 2 minutes. Add chicken and salt and mix them with other ingredients over medium/high heat for 5 minutes. Add stock. When contents reboil, leave them to simmer over low heat (insert asbestos sheet under pan or casserole) for 45 minutes. Add stock cubes, and stir to dissolve. Add peppers, cauliflower, potatoes and milk. Stir contents together until well mixed. Bring to boil, adjust for seasoning with salt. Continue to simmer over low heat for a further 30 minutes, when the dish should be ready. Curried chicken with vegetables can be kept in the refrigerator for 2-3 days and reheated when required. *Serves 10-12.*

5 Curried chicken wings, liver and kidney

Chicken wings, as well as chicken livers and kidneys, are seldom used for any main dish in Western cooking. They can therefore be obtained at less than half the price of meats from other parts of the bird (though the upper part of the wing may often carry a fair amount of good meat). This makes them particularly suitable as materials for Cheap Chow cooking.

675 gr (1½ lb) chicken wings
225 gr (½ lb) chicken livers and kidneys
3 slices root ginger
675 gr (1½ lb) potatoes
4 tomatoes
100 gr (4 oz) green peas
3-4 tablespoons vegetable oil
2 medium onions, finely sliced
3 cloves garlic, crushed
1½-2 tablespoons curry powder
3 tablespoons margarine or lard
3 dl (½ pint) bone or meat stock
1 chicken stock cube

Chop each piece of chicken wing through bone into 2-3 sections. Remove membrane from kidneys and chop with liver into two pieces each. Crush ginger into small grains. Peel potatoes and dice into 2·5-cm (1-in) cubes. Cut each tomato into 4-6 sections. Thaw peas (if frozen).

Heat oil in a large saucepan or casserole. Add onions, garlic, ginger and curry powder. Stir-fry over high heat for 2 minutes. Add the pieces of chicken wings, livers and kidneys and continue to turn and stir-fry for 3-4 minutes. Reduce heat and leave to simmer for 14-15 minutes.

Meanwhile boil the potatoes in a large pan of water for 15 minutes and then drain.

Put margarine or lard in a medium saucepan. Add peas and

turn in the fat for 2 minutes. Add the drained potatoes and turn them for 2 minutes with the peas. Add meat stock, chicken stock cube and salt. Cook over a medium heat for 5 minutes. Pour the contents of the saucepan into the large saucepan or casserole where the wings are cooking. Add the tomatoes. Turn the ingredients over high heat for 2 minutes. Reduce the heat and simmer for a further 5 minutes, when the dish should be ready to serve, with at least an equal weight of bulk food. *Serves 6-8*.

6 Curried fish with vegetables

675 gr (1½ lb) fish (any large chunky fish: cod, haddock, turbot, rock salmon, pike, eel, sea bass, mullet, brill, whale meat, etc.)
3 slices root ginger
550 gr (1¼ lb) potatoes
325 gr (¾ lb) leeks
4-5 stalks spring onions
3 tomatoes
5 tablespoons margarine or lard
2 garlic cloves, crushed
2 large onions, finely sliced
1-1½ tablespoons curry powder
3 dl (½ pint) meat or bone stock
2 chicken stock cubes, crumbled
1·5 dl (¼ pint) milk
2 teaspoons salt
½ lemon

Cut fish into bite-size pieces. Crush ginger into shreds. Peel and cut potatoes into thin slices and parboil for 10 minutes. Cut leeks and spring onions into 3·75-cm (1½-in) pieces; cut tomatoes into quarters.

Heat fat in a large frying pan with lid. Add garlic, ginger, onions, potatoes and curry powder. Stir-fry over high heat for 3-4 minutes, then reduce heat and simmer gently for 5-6 minutes. Add the fish, spreading the pieces evenly over the surface of the pan. Turn them gently until each piece is well covered. Leave to cook for 2 minutes on either side. Pour in the stock, add stock cubes and milk. Bring to boil and simmer for 5 minutes with lid on. Place the tomatoes and sprinkle the spring onions evenly over the other contents. Place the frying pan under the grill and leave for 5 minutes. Adjust seasoning.

Just before serving, squeeze lemon juice over the dish. There should be sufficient spicy food to serve with its own weight of bulk food. *Serves 6-8*.

7 Curried fish and seafood with minced meat and vegetables

This may be a more expensive dish than the previous recipe, but it need not necessarily be so, as some seafoods (such as mussels) are reasonably cheap when in season; this dish should fall well within the scope of Cheap Chow.

325 gr (¾ lb) fish (filleted)
2 tablespoons flour
2·4 litres (4 pints) mussels
3 slices root ginger
225 gr (½ lb) green peas
450 gr (1 lb) cauliflower
3 tablespoons vegetable oil
2 large onions, finely sliced
3 garlic cloves, crushed
325 gr (¾ lb) minced meat
2½ teaspoons salt
1½ tablespoons curry powder
3 tablespoons lard
3 dl (½ pint) meat or bone stock
1 chicken stock cube
4 tablespoons white wine or sherry
1 tablespoon cornflour (blended in 5-6 tablespoons mussel water)

Cut fish into 2·5-cm (1-in) cubes and dust with flour. Clean mussels and parboil in 1·2 litres (2 pints) boiling water for 3-4 minutes. Discard any mussels whose shells have not opened during cooking. Shell mussels and keep 5-6 tablespoons mussel water to blend with cornflour. Crush ginger into shreds. Thaw peas and break cauliflower into individual florets.

Heat oil in large frying pan. Add onions, garlic, ginger and meat; sprinkle with 2 teaspoons salt and 1 tablespoon curry powder. Turn, stir and cook for 5-6 minutes over medium heat. Add cauliflower and peas, stir and cook for a further 5-6 minutes.

Heat lard in a smaller frying pan. Place the fish in the hot fat over medium heat and fry for 1½ minutes on either side. Add mussels and sprinkle contents with remainder of salt and curry. Turn them over gently with the fish for a couple of minutes.

Add the contents of the smaller frying pan into the larger one containing meat and vegetables. Add stock, stock cube and wine. Bring to boil, turning contents over a couple of times, then leave to simmer gently for 5 minutes. Pour in the cornflour/mussel water. Turn the contents over a few times until the liquid parts of the contents thicken.

This makes an extremely savoury dish, weighing nearly 2·5 kg (5¾ lb). Shrimps, prawns, crabs, etc. can be used instead of mussels, when available cheaply in quantity. *Serves 6-8.*

8 Curried eggs with mushrooms, tomatoes and peas

- 6-8 eggs
- 2 slices root ginger
- 225 gr (½ lb) mushrooms
- 3 tablespoons vegetable oil
- 2 garlic cloves, crushed
- 2 medium onions, finely sliced
- 1½-2 tablespoons curry powder
- 1½ teaspoons salt
- 5-6 tablespoons meat or bone stock
- 2½ tablespoons margarine or lard
- 225 gr (½ lb) peas
- 4-5 medium tomatoes, quartered
- 2 tablespoons soya sauce
- 1 teaspoon sugar

Hard-boil the eggs, shell them and cut each into six pieces. Crush ginger into shreds. Remove stalks from mushrooms and cut each cap into quarters.

Heat oil in a large frying pan. Add garlic, ginger, onion, mushroom stalks, curry powder and salt. Stir-fry over high heat for 3 minutes. Add stock, stir and heat for a further 5 minutes. Add eggs, turn them in the curry sauce for 2 minutes, then remove pan from heat.

Heat fat in a saucepan. Add mushrooms and stir-fry over high heat for 2 minutes. Add peas, tomatoes, soya sauce and sugar. Continue to turn and stir-fry for 4 minutes, then add the contents of the saucepan to the frying pan. Stir and mix the ingredients together gently over a high heat for 3 minutes. *Serves 6-8.*

(This is, in fact, a vegetarian dish. For vegetarians, and on meatless days, it is an extremely useful dish to serve with any bulk food.)

Minced meat

In facing up to the problems of budget cookery, sooner or later one has to resort to the use of minced meat. First of all, minced meat is cheaper than most cuts of meat. Secondly, it is easy to combine with other types of inexpensive foods (with vegetables to form savoury dishes, as in Chinese stir-fried dishes, and with bulk foods to form self-contained dishes, as in Shepherd's Pie).

Some of the best ways of making minced meat go further are to cook it in the Chinese or Indian way: with soya sauce or curry.

1 Stir-fried minced meat with soya sauce, mushrooms and green peas

2 slices root ginger
1 chicken stock cube
1 tablespoon cornflour
1·5 dl (¼ pint) warm or hot water
3 tablespoons vegetable oil
2 garlic cloves, crushed
2 large onions, finely sliced
675 gr (1½ lb) minced meat
4-5 tablespoons soya sauce
1 can button mushrooms
675 gr (1½ lb) green peas
2-3 tablespoons red wine (if available)
1 tablespoon chopped parsley

Crush ginger into small shreds. Add stock cube and cornflour to water and blend well.

Heat oil in a large frying pan (with lid) or saucepan. Add garlic, ginger and onions. Stir-fry over high heat for 1½ minutes. Add minced meat and continue to mix and stir-fry for 3-4 minutes. Reduce heat to low and leave to cook for 8-9 minutes, stirring and turning occasionally. Add soya sauce, mushrooms and peas. Turn and mix and leave to cook for another 6-7 minutes.

Add cornflour, stock cube and water mixture. Mix and stir with the other ingredients and leave to cook for a further 4-5 minutes. Pour in the wine and sprinkle with chopped parsley. The dish is now ready to serve: it is especially good with rice or noodles (or spaghetti). *Serves 6-8.*

2 Minced meat baked in marrow with mushrooms

One way of making minced meat go a long way is to bake it in a large marrow, with chopped marrow flesh, peas and mushrooms stuffed inside.

Repeat the previous recipe but use half the amount of peas, and omit canned mushrooms. Add 225 gr (½ lb) chopped fresh mushrooms and some of the marrow flesh. These ingredients for the stuffing should be stir-fried with the minced meat, as were the peas and canned mushrooms in the last recipe.

The marrow selected must be an extra large one. Two sheets of tinfoil will also be required.

Cut the marrow into two, lengthwise, and scoop out the inside leaving a wall approximately 2·5 cm (1 in) thick. Chop about half the scooped-out marrow into cubes. Slice mushrooms, including stalks. Add these marrow cubes and mushrooms to stir-fry with the minced meat during the second stage of the cooking, when peas are added. Sprinkle the contents with 2 additional tablespoons of soya sauce.

Stuff the two halves of marrow (the 'marrow bowls') with minced meat, marrow, peas and mushrooms. Wrap with tinfoil. Stand them in heatproof dishes and place in pre-heated oven, set at 170°C, 325°F, gas 3. Leave to bake for 40-45 minutes. Serve by bringing the marrow bowls to the table. *Serves 6-8.*

For a party, fried rice, Chow Mein, or various soups, etc. can all be served in half a dozen marrow bowls that have been baked in the oven (some items using scooped-out marrows only as containers would need short baking, say, 25-30 minutes). In coastal areas in China, even fish and seafoods are served in marrow bowls. For vegetarians, various vegetable dishes can also be served in these 'bowls'. *Serves 6-8.*

3 Minced meat in cottage pie or shepherd's pie

From marrow bowls to pies may be a step towards the mundane; nevertheless, cooking meat in pies is a very practical way of cooking it.

Repeat the ingredients and quantities of either of the two previous recipes (minus marrow). Grease a very large deep-sided baking dish (preferably one of the French earthenware type). Pour the cooked minced meat and other ingredients into the dish. Cover the meat, etc. with a thick layer of mashed potatoes (675 gr or 1½ lb) with a liberal amount of butter or margarine added. Bake in oven pre-heated to 180°C, 350°F, gas 4 for 35-40 minutes.

As bulk food (potato) is a built-in part of this dish, no further bulk foods will be required. One of its attractions is the convenience of serving it; with wine, soya sauce, sugar, ginger and a chicken stock cube added to the minced meat, its flavour, too, should be most appetizing. *Serves 6-8.*

4 Minced meat pie with eggs, cauliflower and chopped pickles

This pie is cooked with 4-6 hard-boiled eggs, cauliflower (broken into small florets) and 50-100 gr (2-4 oz) chopped sweet pickles. The marrow is omitted. The eggs (chopped into large pieces), cauliflower and pickles should be incorporated and cooked with the minced meat during the second stage of the cooking (refer to recipe 1), when peas are added. The mixture is then put into a well-greased, deep-sided baking dish and covered with 675 gr (1½ lb) of mashed potatoes and baked for 30-35 minutes in an oven pre-heated to 180°C, 350°F, gas 4. The combination of ingredients should make the dish very satisfying and, as with the previous recipe, no further bulk food will be required. *Serves 6-8.*

5 Curried minced meat with marrow, cauliflower, tomatoes and french beans

Most things that can be cooked with soya sauce can also be cooked with curry. Curries are best eaten with rice. Cook the minced meat with a selection of vegetables and serve boiled rice, or one of the varieties of rice provided in the Rice chapter.

225 gr (½ lb) french beans
450 gr (1 lb) cauliflower
2 slices root ginger
1 tablespoon cornflour
1·5 dl (¼ pint) milk
3 tablespoons vegetable oil
2 tablespoons butter or lard
2 large onions, finely sliced
2 garlic cloves, crushed
1½ tablespoons curry powder
450 gr (1 lb) minced meat
1½ teaspoons salt
3 dl (½ pint) stock or water
1 chicken stock cube
225 gr (½ lb) peas
4-5 medium tomatoes, quartered
2 tablespoons soya sauce
1½ teaspoons sugar

Top and tail french beans and cut them into halves diagonally. Break cauliflower into small florets. Crush ginger into small shreds. Blend cornflour with milk.

Heat oil and fat in a large frying pan, or saucepan with lid. Add onion, garlic, ginger and curry powder. Stir-fry them over a medium heat for 2 minutes. Add minced meat and salt. Stir-fry them together for 5 minutes. Pour in the stock and add stock cube, plus all the remaining vegetables. Sprinkle with soya sauce and sugar. Mix vegetables with minced meat. Place a lid over the pan and cook gently over low heat for 15 minutes. Pour in the cornflour/milk mixture. Stir until contents thicken. Serve with plain boiled rice or any of the rice dishes (see chapter 1). *Serves 6-8.*

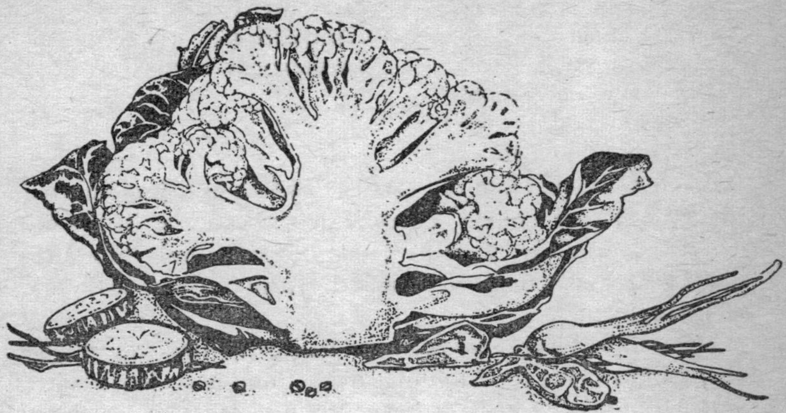

6 Vegetable stews

In China, it is considered essential to use a good stock to make a good vegetable stew. Poultry carcases, meat bones, pigs' trotters, shrimp shells, fish-heads and tails, etc. can all be used to make excellent stocks.

The basic Chinese technique for making good vegetable stew is to fry the large stems of the vegetables in fat for a few minutes over a low heat, then to add the leaves or smaller stems of vegetables, as well as stock. The whole mixture is then simmered.

It is often the practice in China to add a spoonful of dried shrimps or dried mushrooms (which have a very strong flavour) during the early stages of the cooking, to make it more tasty. Here you can add a rasher or two of bacon, cut cross-wise into thin shreds.

These stews often possess a 'sweet-savouriness' (due to fresh vegetables added during the latter stages of cooking) that is often lacking in pure meat dishes – and need not be scorned by any gourmet or connoisseur.

1 Cabbage stew with onions and spring onions

1 large cabbage, white or green
2-3 rashers bacon
2 slices root ginger
2-3 spring onions
2 tablespoons vegetable oil
2 large onions, finely sliced
2 tablespoons lard (or butter, margarine or dripping)
6 dl (1 pint) meat stock
2 chicken stock cubes
2 teaspoons sugar
2 teaspoons salt
2 tablespoons sherry (if available)

Cut out the stem from the cabbage and chop it into approximately 6-8 neat oblong pieces. Cut the cabbage leaves into 2·5-cm (1-in) slices. Cut the bacon crosswise into thin slices. Chop ginger into small grains, and the spring onions into 2·5-cm (1-in) segments.

Heat oil in a large saucepan. Add ginger, onion and cabbage stem, and stir-fry for 2 minutes over a high heat. Reduce heat and leave to cook for 4 minutes more. Add cabbage, bacon and fat. Stir and turn together with the other ingredients until well mixed. Pour in the stock and add stock cubes and sugar. Bring to boil, reduce heat and allow contents to simmer very gently for the next 30-35 minutes. Adjust seasoning, then sprinkle the cabbage with chopped spring onions and the sherry (if available) and serve. Should be eaten with at least its own weight of bulk foods. *Serves 6-7.*

2 Red cabbage stew

Repeat the previous recipe and use red cabbage instead of white or green cabbage. Substitute 4-5 tablespoons of soya sauce for the salt. Add a little red wine (if available), and 1½ teaspoons sesame oil added towards the end will make the stew more aromatic.

For people who like their food 'hot' a couple of chilli peppers (dried or fresh) can be added to the stew during any stage of its cooking. *Serves 6-8.*

3 Marrow stew with tomatoes, peas and potatoes

Marrow, when in season, is probably one of the cheapest vegetables: it can easily be cut into neat, regular sizes, and so is very suitable for making into a Cheap Chow stew.

1·35 kg (3 lb) marrow
550 gr (1¼ lb) potatoes
2 slices root ginger
2 tablespoons vegetable oil
2 garlic cloves, crushed
450 gr (1 lb) peas
2½ tablespoons lard, margarine or butter
9 dl (1½ pints) good meat or bone stock
2 chicken stock cubes
3 tablespoons soya sauce
2 teaspoons sugar
2-3 rashers bacon, shredded
4-5 medium tomatoes, quartered
salt and pepper to taste

Cut the marrow into cubes (discarding skin). Dice potatoes into cubes. Chop ginger into small shreds.

Heat oil in a large saucepan. Add garlic and ginger. Stir a few times and add marrow, potatoes, peas and fat. Turn these around a few times over a high heat. Pour in the stock and add stock cubes, soya sauce, sugar, bacon and tomatoes. Leave contents to simmer gently for 20 minutes after bringing to boil. Adjust seasoning with salt and pepper. Add 1 tablespoon dried shrimps or 2 tablespoons dried mushrooms, also 1 tablespoon sesame oil, if any of these is available.

To eat with bulk foods, as in the previous recipe. *Serves 6-8.*

4 Mixed spring vegetable stew

225 gr (½ lb) young carrots
2 heads of lettuce
225 gr (½ lb) spinach
1 medium cucumber
2 heads of spring greens
225 gr (½ lb) french beans
2 slices root ginger
3 stalks spring onions
3 tablespoons vegetable oil
2 garlic cloves, crushed
325 gr (¾ lb) bean-sprouts
4-5 medium tomatoes, quartered
2 tablespoons lard
9 dl (1½ pints) meat stock
2 chicken stock cubes
salt and pepper to taste
2 teaspoons sesame oil (if available)

Scrape and cut carrots diagonally into 2·5-cm (1-in) sections. Cut lettuce, spinach, cucumber and spring-greens into 2·5-cm (1-in) slices. Top and tail french beans and cut diagonally into 2 sections. Crush ginger into small shreds. Cut spring onion stalks into 1·25-cm (½-in) sections.

Heat oil in a large saucepan. Add garlic, ginger, carrots and stir-fry for 3 minutes over medium heat. Add spring greens and beans, stir for 2 minutes and then simmer at low heat for 5 minutes. Add all the other vegetables, fat, stock, stock cubes and season to taste with salt and pepper. Bring to boil and simmer gently for 15 minutes. Sprinkle with spring onion stalks and sesame oil. Serve this comparatively light stew with bulk food. *Serves 6-8.*

5 Chinese 'hot' vegetable stew

2 red sweet peppers
2 green sweet peppers
2-3 small chilli peppers
1 medium cabbage
1 small red cabbage (or
  4-5 medium tomatoes)
2 slices root ginger
3 tablespoons vegetable oil
2 garlic cloves, crushed
2 medium onions, finely sliced
1 teaspoon salt
2 tablespoons lard
325 gr (¾ lb) bean-sprouts
2 medium gherkins, shredded
9 dl (1½ pints) meat or bone stock
1 chicken stock cube
3 tablespoons soya sauce
1½ teaspoons sugar
pepper to taste

Deseed peppers and cut into 2·5-cm (1-in) slices and the chilli peppers into 1·25-cm (½-in) slices (discard pips). Cut cabbages into 3·75-cm (1½-in) slices (or quarter the tomatoes). Crush ginger into small grains.

Heat oil in a large saucepan. Add chilli peppers, garlic, ginger, onions and salt. Stir-fry over high heat for 2 minutes. Add cabbages, peppers and fat. Mix and turn the ingredients around a few times then leave to cook for 5 minutes. Add the bean-sprouts and gherkins, pour in the stock, stock cube, soya sauce and sugar, and add pepper to taste. Bring to boil and leave to cook over low heat for 10 minutes under cover. Adjust for seasoning and the dish should be ready.

A dish for people who have a taste for food with extra spice and pep. *Serves 6-8.*

6 Stewed vegetables with Chinese transparent (pea-starch) noodles

Chinese transparent pea-starch noodles are an inexpensive but unusual food; their special characteristic is that they are able to absorb a great quantity of liquid when cooked in it; besides they do not become soft or mushy, even when cooked for a long time.

The noodles can easily become as tasty as meat – an important consideration when preparing savoury food to accompany bulk food in Cheap Chow.

To prepare this recipe, use any one of the previous stewed vegetable recipes. Soak 225-325 gr ($\frac{1}{2}$-$\frac{3}{4}$ lb) of transparent noodles in warm water for 3 minutes and strain them. Add the noodles to the vegetable stew with an extra 3 dl ($\frac{1}{2}$ pint) of stock, together with 1-2 teaspoons of sesame oil. Simmer them together for an extra 4-5 minutes. 2-3 tablespoons of gravy from any red-cooked dish would add a great deal to the appeal and succulence of the dish. Dishes with transparent noodles can usually be re-heated but 6 dl (1 pint) of stock should always be added, for by that time the original noodles will have absorbed any extra liquid present in the dish, thus making it much too thick for eating. Indeed, whenever a vegetable or mixed dish is re-heated, it is best to slice up some fresh vegetables, pickles, etc. and have them stir-fried quickly in a small amount of oil (1-2 tablespoons) before adding the left-over dish to the pan along with the stock. This applies to the majority of transparent noodle dishes, especially where red-cooked meat gravy or good stock and some wine is available to be used in the 'enlivening'. *Serves 6-8.*

7 Stewed vegetables with Chinese transparent noodles, bean-curd and braised bamboo shoots

Bean-curd is a staple food consumed in quantity by the Chinese and Japanese, which goes some way in making up the shortage of protein in their diets. It is believed that bean-curd contains more digestible protein than an equivalent weight of beef steak. Bean-curd or Tou Fu can be made at home, but is available from most Chinese food stores and supermarkets. It comes in pale yellow, custard-like cakes. In combination with vegetables, it is often deep-fried, cut into thin slices, then added to the other ingredients that are cooking in the pan, for a short period of stir-frying together. Alternatively, it can simply be added into the pan, to cook with the other ingredients at almost any stage of the cooking. (A little more or less cooking makes no matter.) The addition of an extra tablespoon of soya sauce, wine and

1-2 teaspoons of sesame oil to such a dish would usually enhance its appeal.

In the present case, when Tou Fu is cooked with stewed vegetables (using any of the previous recipes in this chapter), it is best to use 2-3 cakes cut first into 3·75-cm (1½-in) cubes and to add them into the cooking at the same time as the stock. Although Tou Fu is an acquired taste, it is worth cultivating in Cheap Chow cooking, if only for its nutritional value. Braised bamboo shoots are usually available canned, and can be incorporated into any vegetable dish. *Serves 6-8.*

8 Vegetable curry or curried vegetable stew

Take any one of the above vegetable stew dishes – especially recipes 4 and 5 – and add 1-2 tablespoons of curry paste or curry powder into the initial frying with garlic, ginger and onion and before all the other ingredients are added. Both the frying – or stir-frying and cooking – can be prolonged by a minute or two in each instance to give the curry flavour a chance to develop. Since curry has a strong, permeating flavour, it enhances the savouriness of most foods; curry dishes are always excellent for eating with rice.

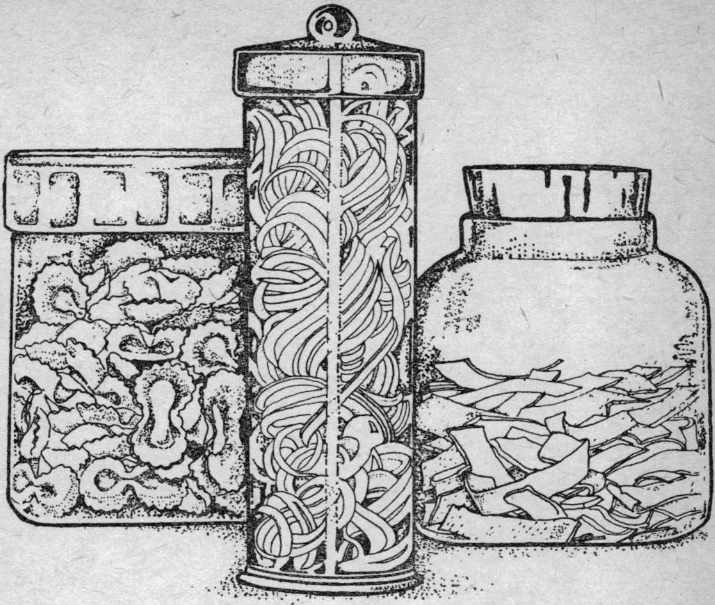

7 Noodles

Noodles have been one of the mainstays of the Chinese diet from time immemorial, especially in northern China. In Western countries noodles can be bought (in various sizes, shapes and forms) from Chinese food stores; or Italian varieties can be used as substitutes. Indeed, it has been said that, in the thirteenth century, Marco Polo brought back these pasta foods from China where he sojourned for no less than nineteen years. If he did bring them back, then he forgot to bring back the Chinese tradition of cooking shredded vegetables with pastas, as we Chinese know it.

The Chinese variety of pasta – noodles – takes about half the cooking time that the Italian pastas need. They are usually served in the following four styles:

soup noodles
sauce noodles
noodles mixed at the table with selected ingredients or 'tossed noodles'
fried noodles or Chow Mein

Noodle soups

Noodle soups are served in China mostly as a meal in themselves, not just as a soup to start off a meal. For the purpose of Cheap Chow, the basic noodle soup can be prepared with the aid of vegetable stew.

For a satisfactory meal, each person should be served a plateful of soup noodles, consisting of approximately 40 per cent noodles, 40 per cent soup and a 20 per cent mixture of vegetables and meat. Where available, a couple of tablespoons of dry sherry, or any wine, can be sprinkled over the dish just before serving, together with ½-1 teaspoon of chilli sauce or Tabasco, for those who like their food 'hot'. Soup noodles based on vegetable stews are excellent on a cold winter's evening. All the vegetable stews in the previous chapter can be adapted, as in the following recipe.

1 Cabbage stew noodle soup

Repeat recipe 1 of the previous chapter (Cabbage stew with onions and spring onions), but use half quantities of ingredients. Boil 675 gr (1½ lb) of Chinese noodles in a large pan of salted water for 5 minutes (or same weight of Italian pasta for 10 minutes). Drain and add to the vegetable stew, together with 9 dl (1½ pints) of extra meat or bone stock, 1½ chicken stock cubes, 1 tablespoon butter or lard and 2 tablespoons soya sauce (or 3-4 tablespoons red-cooked meat gravy, if available). Heat gently together for 9-10 minutes without over-mixing the ingredients – this is left to the diners themselves.

Place the noodles at the bottom of each soup bowl and pour over the soup, arranging the vegetables from the stew on top. Eat with a fork and spoon, or with a pair of chopsticks (in which case the soup is drunk from the bowl). *Serves 3-4.*

2 Noodle soup with red cabbage
Repeat recipe 2 of the previous chapter (page 80), in conjunction with instructions above. *Serves 3-4.*

3 Marrow noodle soup
Repeat recipe 3 of the previous chapter (page 80), in conjunction with instructions above. *Serves 3-4.*

4 Spring vegetable noodle soup
Repeat recipe 4 of the previous chapter (page 81), in conjunction with instructions above. *Serves 3-4.*

5 'Hot' vegetable noodle soup
Repeat recipe 5 of the previous chapter (page 82), in conjunction with instructions above. *Serves 3-4.*

6 Transparent noodles and vegetable soup
Repeat recipe 6 of the previous chapter (page 82), in conjunction with above instructions. (But reduce the ingredients used to one-half and the transparent noodles to a quarter.) *Serves 3-4.*

Note: for noodle soups prepared only from vegetable stews, a dessertspoonful of chopped pickles and a couple of tablespoons of the gravy from red-cooked meat (if available) add interest to the dish. Noodle soups must always rank as among the least expensive of Cheap Chow dishes.

Sauce noodles

Sauce noodles (or noodles in sauce or gravy) differ from noodle soups in China, in that the former are generally served on special occasions (such as birthdays, anniversaries, weddings, etc.) or in restaurants, while the latter are more often served at home.

Sauce noodles, however, can only be satisfactorily prepared with the use of gravy from red-cooked dishes, or by employing a certain amount of master sauce, thus giving this dish a meaty flavour.

For those who like the 'hot' spiciness of curry, various sauce noodles can be made from curry dishes or the leftovers of curry dishes, resurrected by adding a few fresh ingredients to them.

All red-cooked dishes (or leftovers) can be used to make sauce noodles; in this case, add 2-3 tablespoons of soya sauce and 1-2 tablespoons of dry sherry. The following sauce noodle dishes – based on any one of the varieties of soup from the Soup chapter, with some gravy from red-cooked meat, or with sauce from the master sauce incorporated – can all be made along the following lines.

1 Sauce noodles from egg-flower soup

Repeat recipe 1 of the Soup chapter (page 39), adding chicken stock cube and 1·5 dl (¼ pint) of either red-cooked meat gravy or master sauce that has lately been used to cook meat in. Thicken the sauce by adding 1 tablespoon cornflour, blended with 1·5 dl (¼ pint) of extra stock, then heat them together until the soup thickens. 2-3 tablespoons of minced meat, or dried mushrooms (soaked first in warm water for 15 minutes before shredding) can be added at the same time.

Boil 900 gr (2 lb) noodles in salted water for 8 minutes (Italian pasta should be boiled for 15 minutes). Place noodles in individual bowls and pour sauce over. *Serves 5-6.*

2 Sauce noodles from Chinese cabbage soup

Repeat recipe 2 of the Soup chapter (page 39), in conjunction with instructions above. *Serves 5-6.*

3 Sauce noodles from fish-head, onion and watercress soup

Repeat recipe 3 of the Soup chapter (page 40), in conjunction with the instructions above. (The use of fish-head soup as a basis for this recipe for noodles may sound slightly odd to the average housewife in this country, but I can assure readers that this is an established, if not classical, way of producing first-class soup or stock in coastal China.) *Serves 5-6.*

4 Sauce noodles from egg and tomato soup

Repeat recipe 6 of the Soup chapter (page 42), in conjunction with the instructions above. *Serves 5-6.*

5 Sauce noodles from hot and sour soup

Repeat recipe 9 of the Soup chapter (page 43), in conjunction with the instructions above. *Serves 5-6.*

Sauce noodles from red-cooked meat dishes

As we have already seen from the previous recipes, red-cooked meat gravy is used regularly in sauce noodles dishes. Any red-cooked meat dish itself should therefore be an even better base for the making of highly appealing sauce noodles. In the majority of cases only half the quantity of the ingredients stipulated in the recipes of the Red-cooked meat chapter are required for 5-6 portions. To this add 1·2 litres (2 pints) of meat stock, re-inforced with 2-3 tablespoons of soya sauce and 1 chicken stock cube, and thickened with 1½ tablespoons of cornflour.

The mixture should then be simmered over a low heat until the sauce thickens. While the sauce is thickening, boil 900 gr (2 lb) noodles in salted water for 8 minutes (Italian pasta should be boiled for 15 minutes). Place noodles in individual bowls, divide meat among them and pour over sauce. Sauce noodles made from red-cooked meat dishes are about the most satisfying sauce noodles there are, as any true-born Chinese will testify.

All the red-cooked dishes in Chapter 3 can be made into sauce noodles in this manner. Thus:

6 Red-cooked pork sauce noodles

See page 48 and proceed as above.

7 Red-cooked beef sauce noodles

See page 48 and proceed as above.

8 Red-cooked lamb (or mutton) sauce noodles

See page 49 and proceed as above.

9 Red-cooked chicken sauce noodles

See page 49 and proceed as above.

10 Red-cooked fish sauce noodles

See page 50 and proceed as above.

Apart from red-cooked dishes, other types of meat dishes – or simply leftovers of these – can also readily be made into sauce noodles.

11 Sauce noodles from roast meat gravy

Sauce noodles can often be prepared from the materials that are left over in the roasting pan after the beef, lamb or pork has been roasted in it.

225 gr (½ lb) mushrooms
100 gr (4 oz) dried mushrooms
3-4 stalks spring onions
2 tablespoons cornflour
1·2 litres (2 pints) meat or bone stock
675 gr (1½ lb) noodles or Italian pasta
juices from roasting a joint in a pan
3-4 rashers bacon, shredded
50 gr (2 oz) butter
4 tablespoons soya sauce
1½ teaspoons sugar
2 chicken stock cubes
325 gr (¾ lb) bean-sprouts (or shredded celery)
2 tablespoons dry sherry

Cut the mushroom caps into large matchstick shreds, rinse well and discard the stalks. Soak the dried mushrooms in a cup of warm water for 20 minutes, then cut into shreds (retain mushroom water). Cut the spring onions into 2·5-cm (1-in) segments. Mix cornflour with one-quarter of the stock until well blended.

Boil noodles for 10 minutes (Italian pasta should be boiled for 18 minutes) and drain. Rinse under running water to keep separate. Place the roasting pan over medium heat. Add bacon, mushrooms, dried mushrooms and butter. Stir-fry for 2-3 minutes. Pour in the mushroom water, stock and soya sauce, then add sugar and stock cubes. Stir until the stock cubes have dissolved and the liquid in the pan is boiling. Add the bean-sprouts and leave the vegetables and bacon to boil in the gravy for 2 minutes. When the liquid thickens into a sauce, add the noodles. Turn them in the sauce over a low heat for 4-5 minutes until heated through.

Divide the noodles in sauce equally into soup bowls. Sprinkle with chopped spring onions and sherry and serve. *Serves 4-5.*

12 Sauce noodles from roast meat gravy with tomato sauce and eggs

Repeat the previous recipe, but instead of mushrooms use about 325 gr ($\frac{3}{4}$ lb) tomatoes (which, in season, should be inexpensive), 2-3 tablespoons of tomato purée and a couple of eggs.

Beat the eggs up lightly. Cut the fresh tomatoes into slices or wedges and add them to the roasting pan to fry in the oil and gravy for 1-2 minutes before adding the stock, stock cube, soya sauce, sugar and tomato purée. Stir them over a medium heat and cook for 2-3 minutes until thickened. Now pour the beaten egg in a very thin stream, trailing it evenly over the sauce.

The sauce is now ready to be poured over the cooked noodles. If the noodles are cold, they are best added to the sauce and allowed to cook through for a couple of minutes. If sesame oil is available, add $\frac{1}{2}$ teaspoon to each bowl. The addition of beaten eggs produces what we in China call 'egg flowers'. *Serves 4.*

8 Chow T'sai and Chow Mein

Before we proceed to Chow Mein (stir-fried noodles) – the most commonly known Chinese noodle dish served in the West – we shall need, first of all, to deal with stir-frying in general. Chow T'sai (stir-fried dishes) is probably the most common form of cooking in China; and Chow Mein is really only an extension of other stir-fried dishes into which noodles are incorporated. Because stir-frying usually involves the cross-cooking of different materials, it creates the greatest variety of dishes in Chinese cooking.

Chow T'sai

Stir-frying consists mainly of cutting the ingredients into strips, stirring them in a small amount of fat over a high heat, which causes them to be cooked in two or three minutes or less (if too great a quantity of materials is not added into the pan at one time).

Because of the high temperature employed, the softer vegetables should heat through within a minute and become nearly cooked in about two minutes. At this point, to prevent any scorching or burning, a small amount of meat stock is often added, along with any additional liquid flavouring. This should cause a great burst of steam, which, apart from helping to tenderize the foods, will also help to even out the cooking and flavouring of all the ingredients.

The usefulness of stir-frying as a method of cooking lies also partly in its ability to use up small bits and pieces of meat (cooked or uncooked) and partly in the ease with which the resulting dish can be used to combine with all types of bulk food: with noodles to become Chow Mein; with vegetable rice and fried rice as toppings; with pancakes or steamed or toasted buns as stuffings; or as an accompaniment to plain boiled rice or rice-gruel.

Although in stir-frying there is no particular rule as to which meat to cook with which vegetables, it is usually the strongest meats that are combined with the stronger-tasting vegetables: thus beef, mutton, liver, kidney, tripe, etc. usually go with leeks, onions, garlic, ginger, turnips, celery, etc. The more neutral-tasting meats, such as chicken and pork, are cooked with cauliflower, lettuce, mushrooms, peas, sprouts, cabbage, etc. But almost any meat can be cooked and combined with any vegetable in stir-frying; and with the practice of stir-frying at their finger-tips, with whatever odds and ends are available in the kitchen, the Chinese can usually make something out of very little.

1 Shredded pork stir-fried with bean-sprouts and spring onions

325 gr (¾ lb) pork (lean or lean-and-fat)
1 teaspoon salt
3-4 stalks spring onions
2 tablespoons vegetable oil
2-3 tablespoons lard
675 gr (1½ lb) bean-sprouts
3 tablespoons soya sauce
4-5 tablespoons meat or bone stock
1½ teaspoons sugar
pepper to taste

Slice pork into large shreds. Sprinkle and rub with salt. Cut spring onions into 2-cm (1-in) segments.

Heat the oil and fat in a large saucepan. When very hot add pork and stir-fry over high heat for 2 minutes. Add sprouts. Continue to stir-fry over high heat for another 2 minutes until all the sprouts are well lubricated with oil. Pour in the soya sauce, stock and sugar; sprinkle with pepper (to taste). Stir-fry for a further 2 minutes. Sprinkle with spring onions and serve.

This dish is excellent eaten with any plain bulk foods, or in conjunction with Chow Mein (fried noodles) or fried rice. It does not go so well with the wetter dishes, such as rice-gruel (congee) or soup noodles, as the bean-sprouts themselves have a very high water content. *Serves 4-5.*

2 Diced chicken stir-fried with mushrooms and peas

3 teaspoons cornflour
1·5 dl (¼ pint) water
2 slices root ginger
325 gr (¾ lb) chicken meat (breast and any other part of the chicken, or scrapings from the carcase)
225 gr (½ lb) mushrooms
2 tablespoons vegetable oil
3 tablespoons lard
2 garlic cloves, crushed
1 medium onion, finely sliced
1 teaspoon salt
225 gr (½ lb) frozen peas
½ chicken stock cube, crumbled
1 teaspoon sugar

Blend cornflour with half the water. Crush ginger into small shreds. Dice chicken and mushroom caps into small cubes, discarding mushroom stalks.

Heat oil and fat in a large frying pan. Add ginger, garlic and onion. Stir-fry over high heat for ½ minute. Add chicken and salt. Turn and stir them with the other ingredients for 1 minute, still over high heat. Pour in peas and mushrooms, and sprinkle with crushed stock cube and sugar. Add water. Continue the stirring and mixing. Allow the contents to come to a full boil. Reduce the heat and allow ingredients to simmer together for 1 minute. Pour the blended cornflour mixture evenly over the pan. Heat and stir for 1 more minute and serve.

This dish is particularly suitable for eating with all forms of rice dishes: boiled rice, congee (rice-gruel), vegetable rice, fried rice, etc. It can also be served with the majority of noodle dishes. If fried with noodles, the resultant dish becomes 'fried noodles' or Chow Mein. With bulk foods that have already had savoury ingredients incorporated into them, only a small amount of this dish would be needed, perhaps no more than 2-3 tablespoons per portion. *Serves 5-6.*

3 Shredded lamb (or mutton) stir-fried with shredded leeks, bean-sprouts and spring onions

325 gr ($\frac{3}{4}$ lb) lamb (or mutton)
1 teaspoon salt
2 tablespoons flour
3 slices root ginger (or 2 garlic cloves)
4 stalks spring onions
325 gr ($\frac{3}{4}$ lb) leeks
2 tablespoons vegetable oil
4 tablespoons lard
450 gr (1 lb) bean-sprouts
4 tablespoons soya sauce
1·5 dl ($\frac{1}{4}$ pint) meat or bone stock
1$\frac{1}{2}$ teaspoons sugar
1 teaspoon chilli sauce
salt and pepper to taste

Cut lamb into small pieces. Dust and rub with salt and flour. Cut spring onions into 1·25 cm ($\frac{1}{2}$ in) pieces. Crush ginger into shreds. Cut leeks into 3·75 cm (1$\frac{1}{2}$in) slices.

Heat oil and fat in large saucepan. Add ginger and lamb and stir-fry over high heat for 2 minutes. Add leeks and stir-fry for 2 minutes more. Then add the sprouts, soya sauce, stock, sugar and chilli sauce. Mix, and leave to cook for a further 2 minutes. Season with salt and pepper. Stir well, sprinkle with chopped spring onions and serve.

This strong-tasting dish can be eaten with all forms of bulk foods, whether plain or savoury. *Serves 5-6.*

4 Shredded beef stir-fried with onions and spring onions

325 gr ($\frac{3}{4}$ lb) beef
$\frac{1}{2}$ teaspoon salt
1$\frac{1}{2}$ tablespoons flour
3 slices root ginger
5-6 stalks spring onions
3 tablespoons vegetable oil
2 tablespoons lard
2 garlic cloves, crushed
4 large onions, finely sliced
3 tablespoons soya sauce
1$\frac{1}{2}$ teaspoons sugar
3 tablespoons meat or bone stock
2 tablespoons sherry
pepper to taste

Cut beef into small pieces. Dust and rub with salt and flour. Crush ginger into small grains. Cut spring onions into 2·5-cm (1-in) strips. Cut onion into thin slices.

Heat oil and fat in a large saucepan. Add garlic, ginger and onions. Stir-fry over high heat for 2 minutes. Add beef, and mix with the other ingredients for another 2 minutes. Add the soya sauce, sugar, stock and sherry. Continue to stir-fry for 2 more minutes. Just before serving, sprinkle with pepper, to taste, and chopped spring onions. Eat with plain or savoury foods (whether dry or soupy). *Serves 5-6.*

5 Shredded beef with tomato and celery

325 gr (¾ lb) beef
1 teaspoon salt
2 tablespoons flour
3 slices root ginger
450 gr (1 lb) celery
5-6 medium or large tomatoes
3 tablespoons vegetable oil
2 tablespoons lard
1 large onion, finely sliced
4 tablespoons soya sauce
3-4 tablespoons wine (red or white)
½ chicken stock cube

Cut beef into small pieces. Dust and rub with salt and flour. Chop ginger into small shreds. Cut celery into 2·5-cm (1-in) pieces, tomatoes into quarters.

Heat oil and fat in a large frying pan. Add ginger and onion and stir-fry over high heat for 1 minute. Add celery and stir for 1-2 minutes, then push contents to one side of the pan. Add beef to the other side of the pan, stir for 1-2 minutes, then mix with other ingredients. Pour in soya sauce and mix well. Add tomatoes and wine. Sprinkle contents with crushed stock cube, and leave to cook, still over a high heat, for 1-2 minutes, then serve.

The quantity of tomato and celery in the dish gives it a pronounced 'vegetable freshness', whilst the beef, combined with wine and soya sauce, makes it very tasty. Can be eaten with any bulk food. *Serves 5-6.*

6 Stir-fried shredded pork with carrots, cabbage and bamboo shoots

325 gr (¾ lb) lean-and-fat pork
1 teaspoon salt
2 tablespoons flour
1 medium cabbage
325 gr (¾ lb) carrots
225 gr (½ lb) bamboo shoots (optional)
5 tablespoons soya sauce
½ chicken stock cube
3 dl (½ pint) stock (meat or bone)
3 tablespoons vegetable oil
2½ tablespoons lard
1½ teaspoons sugar
1 teaspoon chilli sauce (Tabasco)

Shred the pork into small strips. Dust and rub with salt and flour. Shred the vegetables into roughly 2·5-cm (1-in) pieces.

Place the carrots and bamboo shoots in a small saucepan. Add half the soya sauce, stock cube and stock. Bring contents to the boil and leave to simmer over a low to medium heat for 12 minutes, stirring every 2-3 minutes.

Heat oil and fat in a large saucepan. Add pork and stir-fry over high heat for 2 minutes. Add cabbage and mix well. Add sugar, chilli sauce and remainder of soya sauce. Turn them together a few times and leave to cook over a low heat for 8-9 minutes. Then pour the contents of the small saucepan into the large one. Increase heat to high, stirring well, then simmer for 3 minutes.

This is a slightly saltier dish than most of the previous recipes. It is suitable for serving with bulk foods, particularly with congee (rice-gruel). *Serves 5-6.*

7 Stir-fried curried pork (or chicken) with carrots, potatoes, cabbage and peppers

Repeat the previous recipe, using either pork or chicken or a mixture of the two.

Add 1½-2 tablespoons curry powder to the meat and extend the stir-frying by an extra minute before adding the shredded cabbage and 2 medium peppers cut into thin slices, along with an extra teaspoon of salt. When cooking the carrots substitute potatoes (cut into small wedges) for the bamboo shoots. Simmer for 15 minutes. Combine the contents of the two saucepans and simmer together for 5-6 minutes, then serve.

This curry dish can be eaten with all kinds of bulk foods, including congee (rice-gruel). *Serves 5-6.*

8 Stir-fried shredded beef with transparent noodles, spinach, cauliflower and spring onions

325 gr (¾ lb) beef
1 teaspoon salt
2 tablespoons flour
325 gr (¾ lb) spinach
1 large cauliflower
225 gr (½ lb) transparent noodles
3-4 stalks of spring onions
6 dl (1 pint) meat stock
2 beef stock cubes
3 tablespoons soya sauce
2½ tablespoons vegetable oil
2 tablespoons lard or margarine
1 large onion, finely sliced

Shred the beef into matchstick strips. Dust and rub with salt and flour. Wash spinach and remove the tougher stems. Break cauliflower into florets. Soak noodles in warm water for 5 minutes and drain. Chop spring onion into 1·25-cm (½-in) segments.

Heat stock in a large saucepan. Add stock cubes and stir until dissolved. Add cauliflower and bring to the boil, then simmer for 3 minutes. Add noodles and spinach. Bring to boil again and simmer for 2-3 minutes. Add 1 tablespoon soya sauce and stir.

Meanwhile, heat the oil and fat in a frying pan. Add onion and stir-fry over high heat for 2½ minutes. Add beef and stir-fry for 1 minute. Sprinkle with remainder of soya sauce and spring onions. Continue to stir-fry over high heat for 1-1½ minutes.

Add half the contents of the frying pan into the contents of the saucepan. Stir over low heat for 2 minutes. Pour the contents into a large soup tureen. Garnish with remaining beef and spring onions from the frying pan.

This dish is best served with the drier forms of bulk foods, such as fried rice, vegetable rice or any of the toasted breads or buns, since these transparent noodles absorb a great deal of liquid. *Serves 5-6.*

9 Stir-fried chicken with peppers and pineapple in sweet and sour sauce

The Chinese sweet and sour sauce can be applied to almost any type of stir-fried dish. This is one of the more popular versions.

325 gr (¾ lb) chicken meat (fresh or cooked)
4-5 medium tomatoes
2 medium sweet peppers (1 red)
1 small can pineapple chunks
2 slices root ginger
4 tablespoons vegetable oil
1 large onion, finely sliced
½ teaspoon salt
2 tablespoons soya sauce

For sauce

3 tablespoons sugar
3 tablespoons vinegar
2 tablespoons soya sauce
2 tablespoons cornflour
2 tablespoons tomato purée
3-4 tablespoons orange juice
1·5 dl (¼ pint) pineapple syrup
1·5 dl (¼ pint) water

Mix the ingredients for the sauce in a bowl until well blended. Cut the chicken into small pieces. Cut tomatoes into quarters and peppers into thin slices. Drain pineapple, retaining syrup for sauce. Shred ginger.

Heat 3 tablespoons oil in a large frying pan. Add onion and ginger and stir-fry for 1½ minutes over medium heat. Add chicken, salt, peppers and soya sauce. Continue to stir-fry for 2 minutes, then remove from heat.

Meanwhile, prepare the sauce by heating the balance of the oil in a saucepan. Add tomatoes and pineapple and allow to cook over medium heat for 2 minutes. Stir a few times. Pour the sauce mixture into the pan, raise the heat slightly and stir until the liquid thickens and becomes translucent.

Pour mixture over the chicken and peppers in the frying pan Heat together for ½ minute and serve. Sweet and sour dishes go particularly well with rice, especially the drier versions. *Serves 5-6.*

10 Stir-fried sliced pork with peppers and pineapple in sweet and sour sauce

Repeat the previous recipe, substituting 325 gr (¾ lb) of pork for chicken. In the initial stir-frying, cook the pork for a couple of minutes longer (total: 4 minutes) and also add 1 extra tablespoon of soya sauce.

Sweet and sour pork is particularly suitable for eating with rice dishes, though it can also accompany most pasta dishes, as well as toasted breads and hot buns. *Serves 6-7.*

Chow Mein or fried noodles

The essential Chow Mein consists of cooked noodles, stir-fried with shredded meat and vegetables. The meat and vegetables are shredded, because of the Chinese concept that supplementary ingredients in a dish should be the same shape and size as the main ingredient – in this case, noodles. Thus, in preparing Chow Mein, all the meats and vegetables, whether fresh or dried, raw or cooked, except for peas and prawns, are cut into large matchstick strips.

All the previous stir-fried dishes can be used to make Chow Mein dishes. The following are a few instances, prepared from the stir-fried (Chow T'sai) recipes in the previous section of this chapter.

1 Chow Mein prepared from shredded pork, stir-fried with bean-sprouts and spring onions

Repeat recipe 1 of the previous section of this chapter (page 93). In addition, boil 675 gr ($1\frac{1}{2}$ lb) of noodles or Italian pasta (noodles for 8 minutes, pasta for 15 minutes) and drain. Add 1 extra tablespoon of the oil and fat used in the stir-frying of the pork and vegetables. After a total of 3-4 minutes of stir-frying together, remove half the pork and vegetables from the pan and put aside. Now proceed as before, adding $\frac{1}{2}$-1 chicken stock cube (crumbled) with the liquid, and, when sizzling, pour in the noodles or pasta.

Mix with the oil and gravy and the balance of the meat and vegetables in the pan. Continue stir-frying for 2 minutes over a medium heat until the noodles (or pasta) are thoroughly heated through. Transfer to a well-heated serving dish or divide into individual eating bowls and keep warm. Meanwhile, return the reserved meat and vegetables to the frying pan, with 1 tablespoon of oil or fat. Stir-fry over a high heat, with 1 tablespoon of soya sauce, 2-3 tablespoons stock and 2-3 tablespoons wine (if available), for 1-$1\frac{1}{2}$ minutes.

Use as a heavy garnish on top of the noodles (or pasta). This is a meal in itself and does not need to be served with bulk food. *Serves 4-5.*

2 Chow Mein prepared from diced chicken, stir-fried with mushrooms and peas

Repeat recipe 2 of the previous section (see page 94), in conjunction with instructions above. *Serves 4-5.*

3 Chow Mein prepared from shredded beef, onions and spring onions

Repeat recipe 4 of the previous section (page 95), in conjunction with instructions above. Use a beef stock cube instead of a chicken one. *Serves 4-5.*

4 Chow Mein prepared with shredded beef, stir-fried with tomato and celery

Repeat recipe 5 of previous section (page 96), in conjunction with instructions above. *Serves 4-5.*

5 Chow Mein prepared with shredded pork, carrots, cabbage and bamboo shoots

Repeat recipe 6 of previous section (page 96), in conjunction with instructions above. *Serves 4-5.*

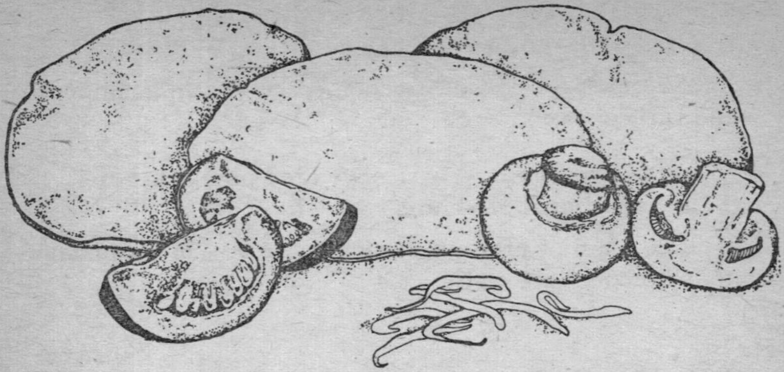

9 Pancakes; yam or potato dishes

Pancakes

Pancakes are a bulk food that can be served stuffed with stir-fried shredded meat and vegetables. Although in the West people are more used to pancakes as a dessert, in China they are as a rule served as savouries. They are frequently called 'spring rolls', being served rolled up into a cylinder, with bottom end turned up, then stuffed with all the vegetables of spring, to mark the advent of the season. As a rule, the stuffing consists of shredded meat, quickly stir-fried with a selection of shredded vegetables. Indeed, any of the Chow T'sai, or stir-fried, dishes (see pages 93-9) can be used as stuffing. A high heat should be maintained throughout, so that the dishes will end up drier than is usual in stir-fried dishes. This is to avoid the sauce dripping out of the pancakes when holding them up to eat.

In the case of the two sweet and sour dishes, the sauce will have to be somewhat thicker – increase the cornflour by 25 per cent and reduce the liquid by 25 per cent. The quantity of vegetables incorporated in the dish can also be increased by 25 per cent, and they should be somewhat more finely shredded than with ordinary stir-fried dishes. The most suitable Chow T'sai, or stir-fried, dishes for use as stuffings for pancakes are:

Shredded lamb and leeks: with slightly more leeks incorporated (see page 95).

Shredded beef with onions and spring onions (see page 95).

Shredded beef with tomato and celery: here the celery should be shredded lengthwise into matchstick shreds like the beef (see page 96).

Shredded pork with carrots, cabbage and bamboo shoots: here again the cabbage, carrots and bamboo shoots should all be shredded lengthwise into matchstick shreds (see page 96).

As for the pancakes themselves, they can be made into a smooth batter by combining an egg with 2½ cups of flour, 2 cups of milk or water and 1 teaspoon of salt. Heat a lightly greased frying pan over low heat until quite hot. Pour a small quantity of the batter (2-3 tablespoons) into the centre of the pan and swirl it around quickly so as to cover the entire bottom of the pan. Cook until the edges of the dough begin to shrink from the sides and the underside is light brown. Toss or turn and cook other side. Pick up the pancake quickly and lay it on a plate, under a damp cloth. Repeat until all the batter is used up, lightly re-oiling the frying pan each time it is used.

In China the wrapping of the spring (pancake) rolls is almost always done by the diners themselves. They are best served with bowls of soup and a bulk food, and are ideal for buffet suppers.

1 Stir-fried shredded pork and egg stuffing for pancakes

325 gr (¾ lb) lean pork
1 teaspoon salt
1½ tablespoons flour
225 gr (½ lb) mushrooms
100 gr (¼ lb) bamboo shoots (optional)
225 gr (½ lb) cabbage (or young leeks)
100 gr (¼ lb) dried mushrooms
4 eggs
6-7 stalks spring onions
4 tablespoons vegetable oil
1½ tablespoons soya sauce
1 teaspoon sugar
3 tablespoons lard
3 tablespoons dry sherry

Shred the pork into matchstick strips. Dust and rub with salt and flour. Shred the mushrooms (discard stalks), bamboo shoots and cabbage into same-size shreds. Soak dried mushrooms for 15 minutes and shred similarly. Beat eggs lightly in a bowl. Cut spring onions into 3·75-cm (1½-in) segments (use all green parts).

Heat oil in a large frying pan. When hot add pork and stir-fry over high heat for 2 minutes. Add mushrooms, bamboo shoots and cabbage and stir-fry for 3 minutes. Add soya sauce and sugar and stir-fry, still over high heat, for 3 minutes more. Remove pan from heat.

Melt lard in a smaller frying pan, and tilt the pan to grease the bottom evenly. Pour in the beaten eggs and reduce heat to low. Leave to cook for 3-4 minutes, or until the eggs have set. Shred the eggs with a knife or fork, and add, together with spring onion stalks, to the pan containing the pork. Pour in the sherry and turn heat up to high. Stir and turn the contents around a few times, then serve.

This dish provides a traditional stuffing for pancakes. *For 18-20 pancakes. Serves 5-6.*

2 Stir-fried cooked meat and vegetable stuffing for pancakes

Any cooked meats can be used very successfully as stuffings for pancakes if they are fried or stir-fried with quantities of vegetables (it is usually best to use one-quarter strong-tasting vegetables, such as leeks, onions or spring onions, with three-quarters bulk vegetables, such as bean-sprouts, shredded cabbage or lettuce).

325 gr (¾ lb) cooked meat
225 gr (½ lb) cabbage
325 gr (¾ lb) leeks
450 gr (1 lb) bean-sprouts
3-4 tablespoons soya sauce
1½ teaspoons sugar
3 tablespoons dry sherry
pepper to taste
3-4 tablespoons vegetable oil
3 tablespoons lard
1½ teaspoons salt

Shred meat and vegetables (where necessary) into large matchstick strips. Mix soya sauce, sugar, sherry and pepper until well blended.

Heat oil and fat in a very large saucepan. Add leeks, cabbage and meat and salt, to stir-fry over high heat for 3½ minutes. Add bean-sprouts, turning them in the hot oil for 2 minutes until all the vegetables are well lubricated. Pour in the soya sauce and stir mixed vegetables a few times, still over high heat for 1 minute, then serve.

This bulk dish of mixed vegetables and meat can be used for stuffing pancakes or in conjunction with bulk foods. *For 18-20 pancakes. Serves 5-6.*

Yam or potato dishes

Anyone who is acquainted with how the poor used to live in China in the bad old days before the Liberation would know that when there was a shortage of rice, people used dried, shredded yams or sweet-potatoes, or more often shredded yam or potato. These were cooked or steamed together with rice (in proportions of one to one or two to one). Frequently meat, vegetables and pickles are added to the bottom of the basin during the steaming; after steaming or double-boiling, the contents are turned out. Then you have a 'pudding' of rice mixed with yam or potato, capped with meat.

1 Rice and potato or yam pudding capped with pork and pickles

325 gr (¾ lb) rice
1 large cauliflower
550 gr (1¼ lb) yams or potatoes
1½ tablespoons lard
325 gr (¾ lb) belly of pork
3 tablespoons vegetable oil or fat
1 large onion, finely sliced
2-3 tablespoons chopped mixed pickles
3 tablespoons soya sauce
3 tablespoons wine or sherry
1½ teaspoons sugar
1 teaspoon salt

Parboil rice in half a saucepan of water for 5-6 minutes and drain. Break cauliflower into individual florets. Cut yam or potatoes into short chips (½ length of ordinary-size chips). Grease a very large and deep basin with lard. Cut belly of pork through skin into small cubes.

Heat oil in a frying pan. Add pork and onion and stir-fry them together for 3 minutes over high heat. Add pickles, soya sauce, wine, sugar and continue to stir-fry together over medium heat for 1½ minutes. Place the pork in the bottom of a large heat-proof basin, skin side down. Pile the onions and pickles on top and pour what gravy there is over them. Arrange the cauliflower in a single layer on top of the pork, etc., then sprinkle with salt and pack a mixture of rice and potato (or yam on top of the cauliflower. Fold a sheet of tinfoil firmly over the top of the basin.

Pour water into a large pan (saucepan or frying pan) to about 5 cm (2 in) deep. Bring to boil and stand the heatproof basin in the water. Leave to simmer gently for 1¾-2 hours, adding more boiling water to the pan whenever necessary.

Serve by turning the contents of the basin out on to a very large, well heated dish. The gravy at the bottom of the basin will seep down over the whole mass of rice and potato *Serves 6-7.*

2 Rice and potato or yam pudding with minced meat

Repeat the previous recipe, using 325 gr (¾ lb) of minced meat instead of belly of pork. Almost any other type of vegetable can, of course, be substituted for cauliflower (especially such vegetables as marrows or aubergines, or a mixture of carrots, turnips, broccoli, beans, peas, etc *Serves 5-6.*

3 Minced meat pudding with broccoli, marrows, rice and potato or yam

As compared with the two previous recipes, using the same ingredients, this is a reverse way of building up the pudding. Pack the parboiled rice and chips of yam or potato in the heatproof basin, pile a layer of vegetables on top, and cover with a thick layer of raw minced meat mixed with one beaten egg. The dish is cooked for 1 hour, in a double-boiler or a saucepan placed inside a larger pan of water, or in an oven heated to 80°C, 350°F, gas 4, with a sheet of tinfoil folded firmly over the top. In this way the savouriness at the top will seep down slowly into the vegetables, rice and yam or potatoes as the cooking proceeds. This 'pudding' is not tipped out when served.

Meat-vegetables-rice-potato puddings were often served in the households of the bourgeoisie in China rather than in those of the formerly poverty-stricken peasants. This may be because minced meat in China, produced by chopping up good cuts of meat, is usually more expensive than belly of pork.

4 Onion cakes

Onion cakes are a simple and popular form of bulk food to accompany meat or savoury dishes in China. They can be eaten on their own when there are no savoury accompaniments available, but are best with a small amount of stir-fried minced meat placed on top: either one of the first two recipes under Minced Meat (see Chapter 5, pages 74–6) should do very well. A heaped tablespoon of cooked minced meat should be enough to go with one onion cake (of course you can have as many tablespoonfuls as you like), so it can be a very economical way of feeding a large number of people cheaply.

225 gr (½ lb) flour
4·5 dl (¾ pint) boiling water
1½ teaspoons salt
5-6 tablespoons finely sliced spring onions
6-7 tablespoons lard

Place the flour in a large mixing bowl. Pour boiling water in gradually, to make a firm dough. Add salt and 2 tablespoons chopped spring onions. Mix and knead for 2-3 minutes, then leave to stand for half an hour. Divide the dough into 12-15 equal parts and shape into cakes roughly 7·5-10 cm (3-4 in) in diameter and 1·25 cm (½ in) thick. Sprinkle half the remaining chopped onion evenly on a flat surface and press the cakes on to them by applying slight pressure. Spread the rest of the chopped spring onions evenly over the board, and turning the cakes over, press them once again on to the onions. In this way the cakes will be studded with chopped onions on both sides.

Heat 4-5 tablespoons of lard in a large flat pan. Tilt the pan so that its surface becomes evenly greased. Spread the cakes out evenly over the pan. Heat over a low-to-medium heat for 2-3 minutes, then turn the cakes over with a fish-slice to heat for a further 2-3 minutes. Add the remainder of the fat into the centre of the pan. Reduce heat to low and fry the cakes for a further 2-3 minutes on each side (total time about 10 minutes). *Makes approximately 12 cakes.*

Each diner should be given two cakes. He eats them by spreading a tablespoon or two of fried minced meat over the cakes; Chow T'sai (or stir-fried dishes) can be used for the purpose. The food can be washed down with tea, beer or soup.

5 Yam or potato croquettes with minced meat and liver

In China we use yams more often than potatoes, but the majority of yam dishes can be prepared equally well with potatoes. These croquettes present another way of using a small amount of minced meat; liver is often incorporated into the minced meat.

1·35 kg (3 lb) yams or potatoes
75 gr (3 oz) butter
2½ tablespoons vegetable oil
2 medium onions, finely sliced
325 gr (¾ lb) minced meat with finely chopped liver
¼ teaspoon salt
2 tablespoons soya sauce
½ teaspoon sugar
100 gr (¼ lb) breadcrumbs
5 tablespoons lard

Boil potatoes or yams for 20-25 minutes. Drain and mash with butter.

Heat oil in a saucepan. Add onion to stir-fry over medium heat for 2 minutes. Add minced meat and liver. Sprinkle with salt, stir well and leave to cook over low heat for 7-8 minutes. Add soya sauce and sugar, and continue to stir and fry for another 5-6 minutes. Divide the minced meat into two portions: one for use as stuffing, and the other to mix with the mashed yams or potatoes.

When both the mashed potatoes and minced meat have cooled somewhat, add one portion of meat to the potatoes. Mash them together until well blended. Form into about 20 egg-shaped balls about twice the size of eggs. Stuff 1½-2 teaspoons of minced meat and liver into the centre of each of the balls and close and smooth the hole over. Sprinkle each ball with breadcrumbs.

Heat the lard in a roasting pan and roll potato balls in the fat until every part of the surface has had contact with the hot fat. Now insert pan into a pre-heated oven set at 180°C, 350°F, gas 4, for 10-12 minutes.

There should be about 3-4 croquettes for each person; they can be eaten with forks. *Serves 5-6.*

6 Yam or potato croquettes with eggs, peas and any left-over meats

Yam or potato croquettes can, of course, also be made with any left-over meats, which are chopped and stir-fried for 2-3 minutes with peas, onions and hard-boiled eggs. The same quantity as in the previous recipe should be made up. *Serves 5-6.*

7 Yam or potato hash with minced meat, peas and onions

It is much more time saving to prepare hash, rather than croquettes. These hashes can be prepared from much the same ingredients as croquettes – the only difference being in their shape.

1·35 kg (3 lb) yams or potatoes
75 gr (3 oz) butter or margarine
3-4 tablespoons milk
225 gr (½ lb) green peas
3 tablespoons vegetable oil
2 large onions, finely sliced
325 gr (¾ lb) minced meat (and liver, or any left-over meat)
2 tablespoons soya sauce
2 teaspoons sugar
1 teaspoon salt

Boil the yams or potatoes for 20-25 minutes and mash them with butter (or margarine) and milk. Thaw peas if frozen.

Heat oil in a frying pan. Add onion, stir-fry for 2 minutes over high heat. Add meat and continue to stir-fry for 3 minutes. Add soya sauce, sugar and salt. Stir-fry for a further 2 minutes. Add peas, to mix with meat and onions. Add the mixture to mashed yam or potato and blend well.

Place the mixture, arranged in half a dozen mounds, in a large heatproof dish. Insert the dish into a pre-heated oven at 180°C, 350°F, gas 4, for 12-15 minutes.

No bulk food is needed with this hash, but it goes very well with a soup or vegetable stew. *Serves 5-6.*

8 Yam or potato hash with meat and vegetables

Repeat the previous recipe. Use in addition 1 medium/large cabbage, cut into 2·5-cm (1-in) pieces.

Stir-fry it with onion and 3 extra tablespoons oil and 1 teaspoon salt, for 3 minutes before adding chopped or minced meat. Then add 1-2 extra tablespoons of soya sauce and proceed as in the previous recipe. *Serves 6-7.*

9 Yam or potato pie with fish

1·35 kg (3 lb) yams or potatoes
3 tablespoons milk
3-4 tablespoons butter or margarine
2 slices root ginger
1 stock cube
7·5 dl (1¼ pints) fish stock
325 gr (¾ lb) fish (any filleted fish or canned tuna)
1 teaspoon salt
2 tablespoons flour
4 tablespoons vegetable oil
2 garlic cloves, crushed
2 medium onions, finely sliced
3 medium tomatoes, quartered
2 tablespoons soya sauce
1 teaspoon sugar

Boil and mash the yams or potatoes with the milk and butter, as in the previous recipes. Crush ginger into small shreds. Dissolve stock cube in stock. Cut fish into 2·5-cm (1-in) cubes. Sprinkle and rub with salt and flour.

Heat oil in a saucepan. Add garlic, ginger, onions and tomatoes. Stir-fry for 1 minute over medium heat and leave to cook for 2 minutes at low heat. Turn the heat up to high and add the fish. Stir well with other ingredients for 2 minutes. Pour in the stock and soya sauce, then add sugar. Turn the fish in the sauce to cook for 1 minute.

Add half the mashed yam or potato into the fish and sauce, and stir until mixed. Heat for 1 minute and transfer to a large heatproof dish. Pile the remainder of the mashed yam or potato on top in an even layer. Place the heatproof dish in a pre-heated oven at 180°C, 350°F, gas 4 for 20 minutes.

This dish is in itself a well-balanced food. It requires no further bulk food to accompany it, but needs such liquids as tea, beer or soup to wash it down. *Serves 5-6.*

10 Soya pork with baked beans and potatoes

550 gr (1¼ lb) belly of pork
1·35 kg (3 lb) new potatoes
½ teaspoon salt
1 chicken stock cube
6 dl (1 pint) bone stock
325 gr (¾ lb) green peas
3-4 tablespoons vegetable oil
3 medium onions, finely sliced
4 tablespoons soya sauce
1 teaspoon sugar
1 can baked beans

Cut pork across lean and fat, through skin, into small cubes. Scrape and clean the potatoes. Add salt and stock cube to stock. Thaw peas (if frozen).

Heat oil in a large casserole. Add onion and pork and stir-fry over high heat for 4-5 minutes. Add soya sauce, sugar and a quarter of the stock. Bring to boil and leave to simmer in a pre-heated oven at 170°C, 325°F, gas 3, for 1¼ hours.

Cook the potatoes in the remainder of the stock in a saucepan for 10 minutes. Add peas and beans and cook together for a further 10 minutes. Add contents of saucepan to casserole, keeping ingredients somewhat separate. Return the casserole to the oven to cook slowly for another 20 minutes.

This is another fairly well balanced dish, and requires no further bulk food. *Serves 6-7.*

11 Curried pork with broad beans, peas and potatoes

Repeat the previous recipe, but substitute sliced broad beans for baked beans. And instead of using soya sauce, use 2-3 table-spoons of curry powder or paste with 2 teaspoons salt to stir-fry with the onions for 2 minutes before adding the pork. Fry the pork for 5 minutes with the curry and onion and leave to simmer gently for 10 minutes before adding 325 gr (¾ lb) broad beans – cut diagonally into 2·5-cm (1-in) wide strips – and half of the stock. Leave the contents to simmer gently for 40 minutes.

Scrape and prepare the potatoes (if not new, these should be diced into 3·75-cm (1½-in) cubes and boiled for 5 minutes, then drained). Simmer the potatoes and peas in the remainder of the stock in a saucepan for 15 minutes. Stir every 5 minutes.

Pour the contents of the saucepan into a casserole, keeping the ingredients somewhat apart. Insert an asbestos sheet under the casserole and leave to simmer for a further 20 minutes over a low heat. *Serves 6-7.*

10 Egg dishes

Eggs are, of course, one of the most widely available and used items of food in the world. They have three other important advantages over many other foods; namely that they are relatively inexpensive, keep well and can be cooked in a reasonably short time.

In China, eggs are most frequently steamed or stir-fried; and the number of dishes that can be prepared from them is almost endless. Steamed egg dishes are really savoury custards, where eggs are first lightly beaten and blended with flavoured stock; then whatever other ingredients are available are chopped and further blended into them.

Stir-fried eggs are not unlike Western scrambled eggs, but in the Chinese method, the beaten eggs, when cooked in hot fat, are allowed to set and then are lightly turned and broken up into small pieces. They can be mixed with almost any other type of ingredient, to produce distinctive dishes.

It happens that soya sauce goes very well with eggs; but it should never be cooked with the eggs themselves, just sprinkled on at the last moment. Two other types of ingredients, chopped spring onions and dry sherry (or the Chinese 'Yellow Wine'), combine exceedingly well witn eggs cooked in this mannei, in making them both more appealing and more aromatic. When all three – soya sauce, chopped spring onions and sherry – are used together, then even a very ordinary stir-fried egg can become a dish for the connoisseur. Yet the cost of these ingredients need not add up to as much as 40p for the whole dish. Here are a few examples of stir-fried egg dishes, which should hint at the vast number of dishes that exist in the Chinese repertoire.

Stir-fried egg dishes

1 Stir-fried eggs with cucumber, spring onions (scallions) and mushrooms

6 eggs
1½ teaspoons salt
4 stalks spring onions
⅓ medium size cucumber
325 gr (¾ lb) mushrooms
3 tablespoons lard
1 medium onion, finely sliced
3 tablespoons vegetable oil
2-3 tablespoons sherry
1 tablespoon sesame oil (optional)
pepper to taste
2½ tablespoons soya sauce

Beat the eggs and salt with a fork for 8-10 seconds. Cut spring onions into 1·25-cm (½-in) segments. Dice cucumber (including skin) into 1·25-cm (½-in) cubes. Remove stalks of mushrooms and cut larger caps into quarters. Wash well.

Heat lard in a large frying pan. Add onion and mushrooms and stir-fry over medium heat for 2 minutes and leave to fry over low/medium heat for 3 more minutes. Add cucumber and stir-fry together over high heat for 1 more minute, then remove from heat.

Heat oil in a smaller frying pan. When hot add the beaten eggs. When they have nearly set, give them a stir to break the eggs up into small pieces.

Add the eggs to the mixture in the large frying pan. Turn the heat up high and sprinkle the contents with spring onion, sherry and sesame oil. Stir the contents a few times (about 15 seconds), adjust seasoning, then transfer to a large well-heated serving dish, sprinkle with soya sauce and serve with bulk food. *Serves 6-7.*

Note: butter or margarine can be used in place of lard.

2 Stir-fried eggs with onions, tomatoes and peas

6 eggs
1½ teaspoons salt
3 tablespoons lard
2 medium onions, finely sliced
5-6 medium tomatoes, quartered
325 gr (¾ lb) frozen peas
3 tablespoons vegetable oil
2 tablespoons dry sherry
1 tablespoon sesame oil (optional)
3 stalks spring onions, finely sliced
pepper to taste
2½ tablespoons soya sauce

Beat eggs with salt for 8-10 seconds.

Heat lard in a large frying pan. Add onion and stir-fry over medium heat for 2 minutes. Add tomatoes and peas. Mix with onion in the hot fat and leave to fry for 2 minutes more over medium heat. Remove from heat.

Heat oil in a smaller frying pan and add beaten eggs. Cook over low/medium heat until the eggs have nearly set. Stir, then break the eggs, when nearly set, into small pieces.

Add eggs to large frying pan. Sprinkle with sherry, sesame oil and spring onions. Stir the contents and adjust seasoning over high heat.

Transfer to a well-heated serving dish. Sprinkle evenly with soya sauce and serve with bulk foods. *Serves 6-7.*

3 Stir-fried eggs with minced meat, sweet peppers and celery

1 red and 1 green medium sweet pepper
325 gr (¾ lb) celery
1½ teaspoons salt
pepper to taste
6 eggs
3 tablespoons lard
2 medium onions, finely sliced
225 gr (½ lb) minced pork
1 teaspoon sugar
4 tablespoons soya sauce
4 tablespoons vegetable oil
3 tablespoons dry sherry
1 tablespoon sesame oil (optional)

Deseed and cut peppers into 1·25-cm (½-in) slices. Cut celery diagonally into 1·25-cm (½-in) segments. Add salt and pepper to eggs and beat with a fork for 8-10 seconds.

Heat lard in a large frying pan. Add onion and pork and stir-fry over a high heat for 3 minutes. Add celery. Mix and cook for 3 minutes over a medium heat. Sprinkle with sugar and soya sauce, and remove from the heat.

Heat oil in another large frying pan. Add peppers and stir-fry for 2 minutes, then push to one side of the pan. Pour the beaten eggs into the other side of the pan. Leave over low heat until the eggs have nearly set. Stir to break up the eggs into small pieces.

Add the eggs and peppers to first pan and mix over a high heat for 1 minute. Sprinkle with sherry and sesame oil, adjust seasoning and stir a couple of times. Then transfer the contents, which should now be highly savoury and aromatic, on to a large, well-heated serving dish. Eat with bulk foods. *Serves 6-7.*

4 Stir-fried eggs with chopped bacon and vegetables

6 eggs
1½ teaspoons salt
pepper to taste
4 rashers bacon
5 tomatoes
1 large cauliflower
3 tablespoons lard
2 medium onions, finely sliced
1 chicken stock cube, crumbled
3 tablespoons vegetable oil
225 gr (8 oz) peas
3 tablespoons soya sauce
2 tablespoons sherry (optional)
1 tablespoon sesame oil (optional)

With a fork, beat eggs, with salt and pepper, for 8-10 seconds. Cut bacon into thin strips and each tomato into 6 wedges. Break cauliflower into small individual florets, then parboil for 3 minutes and drain.

Heat fat in a large frying pan. Add onion and bacon and stir-fry over high heat for 2 minutes. Add tomatoes and cauliflower. Sprinkle with powdered stock cube and turn the contents over two or three times. Place a lid over the pan, reduce heat to low. Allow the contents to cook for 3 minutes. Remove from heat.

Heat oil in a smaller frying pan over medium heat. Add peas, stir two or three times then push them to one side of pan. Pour the beaten eggs into the other side of the pan. Heat until the eggs have nearly set. Stir and break the eggs into 2·5-cm (1-in) pieces.

Add the eggs and peas into the larger frying pan containing the other vegetables. Sprinkle the contents with sherry and sesame oil. Increase the heat to high. Turn the contents over two or three times.

Transfer the contents into a large, well-heated serving dish, sprinkle with soya sauce and serve. To eat with any bulk food. *Serves 6-7.*

5 Stir-fried eggs with buttered carrots, peas and marrows

1½ teaspoons salt
pepper to taste
6 eggs
2 rashers of bacon
325 gr (¾ lb) young carrots
325 gr (¾ lb) marrow
225 gr (½ lb) peas
1 chicken stock cube
4 tablespoons butter
3 tablespoons vegetable oil
3 tablespoons soya sauce
1 tablespoon sesame oil (optional)

Add salt and pepper to eggs and beat for 8-10 seconds. Cut bacon into thin strips. Scrape carrots and dice into small wedges. Cut marrow into 2·5-cm (1-in) cubes. Parboil carrots in boiling water for 3 minutes, add marrow and parboil for 2 further minutes. Drain thoroughly. Thaw peas if frozen. Crush stock cube.

Heat butter in a roasting pan. Add carrots and stir-fry for 1 minute over medium heat. Add marrow, peas, bacon and stock cube and turn with the carrots for 2 minutes until all the vegetables are well greased. Insert the roasting pan into a moderate oven (180°C, 350°F, gas 4) for 10 minutes.

Heat oil in a large frying pan and add beaten eggs. When nearly set, break the eggs up into 2·5-cm (1-in) pieces. Tip contents of roasting pan into frying pan. Turn the heat high and stir contents a few times, adjusting seasoning if necessary. Transfer to a well-heated dish. Sprinkle with soya sauce and sesame oil, then serve with any bulk food. *Serves 6-7.*

6 Stir-fried eggs and vegetables with sweet and sour sauce

The Chinese think that sweet and sour sauce goes well with almost any egg dish, including those used in this chapter. Here is an example of one:

6 eggs
1½ teaspoons salt
pepper to taste
1 large cauliflower
2 tablespoons lard
1 medium onion, finely sliced
4-5 medium tomatoes, quartered
3 tablespoons vegetable oil

For sauce

1½ tablespoons cornflour blended in 6 tablespoons water
2½ tablespoons vinegar
2 tablespoons sugar
1½ tablespoons tomato purée
1½ tablespoons soya sauce
4-5 tablespoons orange juice
1·5 dl (¼ pint) water

Mix the sauce ingredients in a bowl until well blended. Heat and stir the mixture in a small saucepan over medium heat until it thickens and is translucent. Beat eggs with salt and pepper for 8-10 seconds. Break cauliflower into small individual florets, parboil for 3 minutes and drain.

Heat lard in a large saucepan. Add onion, stir-fry over a high heat for 1 minute. Add cauliflower and stir with onion for 3 minutes. Add the tomatoes and mix with contents for 2 minutes, then remove from heat.

Heat oil in a frying pan and pour in the beaten eggs. Cook over a low heat until the eggs have nearly set. Stir to break up the eggs into small pieces. Add the eggs to the saucepan.

Mix well for 1 minute over a high heat, then transfer on to a well-heated serving dish.

Return the saucepan containing the sauce over medium heat for half a minute. When hot and bubbling pour it over the dish and serve. Eat with any bulk food; all rice dishes are particularly suitable. *Serves 5-6.*

Scrambled egg dishes

7 Chinese scrambled-egg pudding

This is a characteristic North China dish, popular for eating with rice.

6 eggs
1½ teaspoons salt
pepper to taste
1½ chicken stock cubes
3 dl (½ pint) meat stock
1½ tablespoons cornflour
100 gr (¼ lb) chopped ham
4 stalks spring onions
3 tablespoons lard
3 tablespoons butter or margarine
2 tablespoons soya sauce
2 tablespoons dry sherry

Beat eggs with salt and pepper for 8-10 seconds. Crumble stock cubes and dissolve over a medium heat in stock thickened with cornflour. When wholly dissolved leave mixture to cook gently for 1 minute. Allow to cool somewhat, then add the beaten egg and blend all together to make a smooth mixture. Chop the ham and spring onions into small pieces.

Heat lard and butter in a large saucepan over a medium heat and pour beaten egg-and-stock mixture into the saucepan, in a thin stream, stirring all the time with a wooden spoon in one direction until the mixture becomes thick and pudding-like. Sprinkle with chopped ham, soya sauce, spring onions and sherry, then stir a few times until all the ingredients are heated through.

Transfer the egg pudding into a large serving bowl, and serve with any dry form of bulk food (the dish was originally invented to go with rice, which often requires a moist accompaniment). *Serves 5-6.*

8 Chinese scrambled-egg pudding with smoked or fresh fish

1½ chicken stock cubes
3 dl (½ pint) stock (meat or bone)
6 eggs
1½ teaspoons salt
1½ tablespoons cornflour
3 rashers of bacon
2-3 anchovy fillets
225 gr (½ lb) smoked haddock (or any filleted fish)
4 stalks spring onions
4 tablespoons lard, butter or margarine
3 tablespoons vegetable oil
1 large onion, finely sliced
2 garlic cloves, crushed
2 tablespoons sherry

Dissolve stock cubes in warm stock and allow to cool. Beat egg with salt for 8-10 seconds. Mix with stock and cornflour until well blended. Chop bacon and anchovy into small slivers. Boil smoked or fresh fish for 5 minutes. Drain and flake. Cut spring onions into 1·25-cm (½-in) segments.

Heat fat and oil in a large saucepan. Add chopped onion, garlic and bacon and stir-fry together for 1½ minutes. Pour in the egg/stock mixture in a thin stream, stirring all the time. When the contents have thickened into a pudding, sprinkle with flaked fish and anchovy. Reduce the heat and sprinkle spring onions and sherry evenly over all.

Serve with all rice dishes, hot cakes, toasted buns and breads – also with pasta dishes. *Serves 5-6.*

9 Chinese scrambled-egg pudding with cheese and peas

Repeat the previous recipe. Instead of smoked fish and anchovies, use 225 gr (½ lb) shredded or grated cheese and 325 gr (¾ lb) green peas. Stir them into the egg/stock/cornflour mixture after this has thickened into a pudding. Leave to cook gently over a low heat for a couple of extra minutes. Sprinkle with the sherry, chopped spring onions and add 1½ tablespoons soya sauce during the last half-minute of simmering. *Serves 5-6.*

Steamed egg custards

10 Steamed savoury egg custard

Savoury egg custards are another accompaniment for rice dishes in China. They can probably be prepared even more cheaply than egg puddings, or stir-fried egg dishes.

2 chicken stock cubes
1 litre (1¾ pints) stock (meat or bone)
3-4 eggs
1 tablespoon vegetable oil
1½ teaspoons salt
3 stalks spring onions
2 tablespoons sherry
pepper to taste
2½ tablespoons soya sauce

Dissolve stock cubes in warm stock and leave to cool. When cool combine with beaten eggs, oil, salt, chopped spring onions, sherry and pepper to taste. Mix all together until well blended.

Place the mixture in a large Pyrex dish or any deep-sided heatproof dish. Place the dish in a steamer and steam for 25 minutes – or cover the top of the dish with a large sheet of tinfoil and place in a pre-heated oven at 180°C, 350°F, gas 4, standing in a roasting pan containing 3·75 cm (1½ in) boiling water, for 30 minutes. Although steaming is preferable to baking, the average Western household kitchen is more often equipped with an oven than a steamer.

Sprinkle the top of the custard with soya sauce and serve. Savoury custards are usually eaten in conjunction with fried, vegetable or plain boiled rice. *Serves 5-6.*

11 Fancy egg custard with minced meat

Repeat recipe 10, but add cooked minced meat or any left-over cooked meat finely chopped or minced. Blend into the egg/stock mixture and steam or bake for 25-30 minutes. When ready to serve sprinkle with 2 tablespoons of minced ham and soya sauce. *Serves 5-6.*

12 Fancy egg custard with seafood

The majority of fish or other seafoods are comparatively expensive these days, but when in season some can be reasonably priced enough for Cheap Chow dishes. Canned fish such as tuna can also be used.

Repeat recipe 10, but double the quantity of spring onions and salt. Add 225 gr (½ lb) canned tuna; or boil smoked haddock or any smoked fish or fresh fish for 5-6 minutes. Then drain and mix with half the chopped spring onions and 3 teaspoons salt.

Leave the fish to season for 30 minutes, then add to the egg/stock mixture. Blend together until the fish is well mixed, then place in a Pyrex or other heatproof dish and steam for 25 minutes or bake for 30 minutes, as in recipe 10. Serve as before by sprinkling with the balance of the chopped spring onions and soya sauce when the dish is brought to the table. *Serves 5-6.*

13 Savoury egg custard with vegetables

The vegetables used can be peas, beans, mushrooms, tomatoes, water chestnuts, sweet peppers, spinach, spring onions and a couple of spoonfuls of mixed pickles. The larger vegetables should be diced into small pieces. The usual procedure is to divide the vegetables into two parts: mix half into the egg/stock mixture to steam or bake (the harder vegetables will need 3-5 minutes' parboiling first). Use the remaining half to stir-fry with 2 tablespoons of oil or butter, with the addition of some soya sauce, sugar and wine, for a matter of 2-3 minutes. When cooked use this stir-fried mixture to garnish the custard just before serving. *Serves 5-6.*

All three types of fancy savoury egg custard (recipes 11, 12, 13) are excellent with bulk rice dishes, especially the drier ones such as fried rice.

11 Dishes using sesame oil and paste, bean-curd and soya sauce

Sesame oil or paste dishes

In Chinese food there is a whole series of dishes employing sesame oil and paste as the principal flavouring agents. When blended with a small amount of soya sauce, sugar, wine and concentrated chicken stock, and aromated with chopped spring onions (or chives) and garlic, they combine to produce an exceptionally palatable and satisfying flavour. In Chinese cooking sesame oil and paste is also used in conjunction with meats and vegetables, or such bulk foods as rice and pasta. In the West, sesame paste may not always be readily available, but peanut butter can be used as a substitute (though nowadays sesame paste – often called Tahina – is available from health food stores). The correct proportion is 2 units of sesame oil to 4 units of water and 5 units of sesame paste or peanut butter, with a small amount of salt, to taste.

To complete the composition, we Chinese often add 1 unit of

soya sauce, 1 unit wine or sherry, 1 unit peanut oil (or clarified butter or lard), ½ unit sugar and ½ unit chopped spring onions. When served with pasta – especially the boiled or steamed types – this sauce is tasty eaten with vegetables. Thus:

1 Basic tossed noodles with sesame oil/paste

- 450 gr (1 lb) noodles or Italian pasta
- 1½ tablespoons peanut (or corn) oil
- 3-4 tablespoons sesame paste or peanut butter
- 2½ tablespoons water
- 1½ tablespoons soya sauce
- 1½ teaspoons sugar
- 2 tablespoons sherry
- 1½ tablespoons sesame oil
- 1½ teaspoons chopped chives
- 1 teaspoon salt

Boil the noodles or pasta (5 minutes for the former and 10 minutes for the latter). Drain quickly and while still hot place in individual bowls and sprinkle peanut oil (or melted butter and salt) on to them to prevent their sticking together. Mix the peanut butter, water, soya sauce, sugar, sherry and sesame oil together into a paste. Place a large dollop on top of individual portions of pasta and sprinkle with chopped chives and salt.

Here the tossing is left to the diners themselves. In spite of its simplicity the dish has an amazing appeal, and for cheapness there are few to beat it. *Serves 3-4.*

2 Tossed noodles with sesame oil/paste and other ingredients

Repeat the previous recipe. In addition to the ingredients used, add 4 tablespoons concentrated chicken stock (by dissolving ½ chicken stock cube in 4 tablespoons warm water), ¾ teaspoon chilli sauce (Tabasco) and ¾ teaspoon Marmite, heat through in a small saucepan and toss with the noodles. *Serves 3-4.*

3 Tossed noodles with sesame oil/paste and a variety of vegetables

The vegetables should be shredded and placed in individual bowls or dishes on the table. The most popular ones used for this purpose are bean-sprouts, celery, cabbage, young carrots, cucumber, lettuce, watercress and mustard and cress. They can be served blanched or raw. In addition, a few sauce dishes containing vinegar, soya sauce, mustard, chilli sauce and chopped pickles as well as chutney and peanut butter (blended with an equal amount of salad oil) should be placed on the table for the diners to use as supplements to incorporate along with their vegetables. The noodles are just plain boiled.

Sesame oil/paste is seldom applied directly to rice, but to meats, vegetables and bean-curds or other ingredients, which are in turn eaten with the rice. It is usually applied to stir-fried dishes, which are quickly cooked, and is rarely used in long-cooked dishes.

4 Shredded stir-fried pork with sesame oil/paste and spring greens

325 gr (¾ lb) pork (lean and fat)
1 kg (2¼ lb) spring greens
1·5 dl (¼ pint) chicken stock
1 chicken stock cube
2½ tablespoons butter
3 tablespoons vegetable oil
2 tablespoons soya sauce
1 tablespoon sugar
2 tablespoons wine
3 tablespoons sesame paste (or blend 2 tablespoons peanut butter with 1½ tablespoons water and ¾ tablespoon sesame oil)

Cut pork into shreds. Cut greens into 3·75-cm (1½-in) slices, parboil for 3 minutes and drain.

Heat chicken stock, stock cube, butter and greens for 5 minutes over high heat, then remove from heat.

Heat oil in a frying pan. Add shredded pork and stir-fry over high heat for 4 minutes. Add soya sauce, sugar and wine. Stir-fry for a further 2 minutes. Reduce heat and add sesame paste (or peanut butter blended with water and sesame oil).

Spread the spring greens evenly over a large serving dish. Pile the stir-fried pork in sesame paste in the middle of the greens. Use as a savoury accompaniment to bulk foods, such as rice, rice dishes or noodles. *Serves 4-5.*

5 Sliced liver in sesame paste with cauliflower

In China both liver and kidneys (lamb, pork or beef) are used for this dish. Here one has only to repeat the previous recipe, substituting liver and/or kidneys for pork. The liver (or kidneys) should be cut into slivers about 3·75-cm (1½-in) long and 2-3 times the thickness of matchsticks.

They need to be stir-fried for not more than 1½ minutes, but the heat will have to be high and the oil very hot when the meat is added. A small amount of crushed garlic and ginger might be added to the oil before stir-frying. The sesame paste should be added immediately after removing the pan from the heat. In this instance the cauliflower is cooked in precisely the same manner as the spring greens were cooked in the previous recipe (breaking the cauliflower up into small florets and cooking them for 5 minutes).

Spread the cauliflower evenly over a large serving dish. Pile the stir-fried liver and kidney with sesame sauce at the centre. Serve with bulk foods, such as rice, noodles, toasted buns and onion cakes. *Serves 4-5.*

6 Braised stir-fried tripe in sesame paste with spinach and noodles

900 gr (2 lb) noodles or Italian pasta
550 gr (1¼ lb) spinach (or watercress)
4 tablespoons butter
1 teaspoon salt
2 slices root ginger
900 gr (2 lb) tripe (pork or beef)
4 tablespoons vegetable oil
2 medium onions, finely sliced
2 garlic cloves, crushed
4 tablespoons soya sauce
1½ teaspoons sugar
3-4·5 dl (½-¾ pint) red wine
3-4 tablespoons sesame paste

Boil noodles for 10 minutes (pasta for 20 minutes). Cut spinach into 3·75-cm (1½-in) slices (removing tough parts) and add into the pan to boil with noodles or pasta for a further 5 minutes. Drain and toss with butter and salt. Crush ginger into small shreds. Plunge tripe into boiling water; boil for 5 minutes, then drain. Slice with sharp knife into slivers.

Heat oil in a saucepan and stir-fry onion, garlic and ginger in it for 1 minute. Add tripe and mix with hot oil and other ingredients over a high heat for 3 minutes. Add soya sauce, sugar and wine. Stir well and reduce heat to low. Insert an asbestos sheet under the pan and leave to simmer very gently under cover for 1 hour, stirring every 15 minutes. Remove lid and cook for a further 30 minutes. Add sesame paste (or 3 tablespoons peanut butter blended with 1½ tablespoons water and 1 tablespoon sesame oil). Combine the mixture quickly with the tripe.

Spread the noodles (or pasta) and spinach evenly over a well-heated serving dish, then turn the tripe and onions on to the centre of the noodles. *Serves 6-8.*

Tou Fu or bean-curd

Tou Fu, or bean-curd, is one of the staple foods of China (and Japan). It also happens to be one of the most nourishing foods, as well as one of the cheapest. Tou Fu usually comes in approximately 5- × 2·5- × 7·5-cm (2- × 1- × 3-in) cakes, with a texture like firm custard or junket. It is chalky-white in colour and without much flavour in itself; it is largely an acquired taste. Although not worth more than 5-15p a piece, so sought after is it that some Chinese or Japanese would spend £1 on a taxi fare to visit a place where Tou Fu is available and well cooked.

A sauce (such as minced meat, sesame paste, bean paste, black-bean, Tabasco) is poured over the Tou Fu, to make it more tasty. It can be eaten with quantities of plain boiled rice, or rice-gruel, particularly when supplemented by a vegetable dish or vegetable stew. This makes a well-balanced meal, containing protein (bean-curd), minerals and vitamins (vegetables) and carbohydrates (rice).

1 Minced meat and Tou Fu balls

3 cakes Tou Fu
100 gr (¼ lb) minced meat
1 egg
½ teaspoon salt
4 tablespoons soya sauce
2 tablespoons cornflour
pepper to taste
1 large cabbage
oil for frying
3 tablespoons butter
1 large onion, finely sliced
1 chicken stock cube, crumbled

Cut Tou Fu into very small pieces. Mix it in a bowl with minced meat, egg, salt, 2 tablespoons soya sauce, cornflour and pepper. Form the mixture into meatballs. Cut the cabbage into 2·5-cm (1-in) slices.

Heat oil in a frying pan, add 2 meatballs at a time – to fry until slightly brown. Drain and put aside.

Heat butter in a casserole and gently fry the onion. Add cabbage, turn it in the butter and sprinkle with powdered stock cube. Spread the cabbage evenly over the bottom of the casserole. Arrange the meatballs on top of the cabbage. Pour remainder of soya sauce on top of meatballs. Insert casserole into a pre-heated oven at 150°C, 300°F, gas 2 for 1 hour. To be eaten with any bulk food. *Serves 5-6.*

2 Plain Tou Fu with sesame paste, soya sauce and chilli sauce

5-6 cakes Tou Fu
3 tablespoons sesame paste
5 tablespoons soya sauce
3 tablespoons peanut oil
1½ teaspoons chilli sauce
2 teaspoons sugar
1 tablespoon vinegar

Poach bean-curd (Tou Fu) in boiling water for 2 minutes. Drain and arrange in the centre of a large serving dish. Mix sesame paste, soya sauce, oil, chilli sauce, sugar and vinegar into a sauce. Pour the sauce evenly over the pieces of Tou Fu and serve. *Serves 5-6.*

3 Stir-fried mashed Tou Fu with minced meat and peas

225 gr (½ lb) mushrooms
1 tablespoon cornflour
3 dl (½ pint) stock
4 cakes Tou Fu
3 tablespoons vegetable oil
2 medium onions, finely sliced
225 gr (½ lb) minced meat
3 tablespoons soya sauce
1½ teaspoons sugar
pepper to taste
225 gr (½ lb) green peas
1 chicken stock cube
2 tablespoons butter
1 teaspoon salt

Clean and cut mushroom caps into thin strips (discard stalks). Blend the cornflour with half the stock. Cut and mash the bean-curd.

Heat oil in a large frying pan. Add onions and minced meat. Stir over high heat for 2 minutes. Add soya sauce, sugar, pepper, and continue to stir-fry for 2 minutes over medium heat. Add mushrooms, peas, balance of stock, stock cube and butter. Stir until well mixed and leave to simmer together for 5-6 minutes. Add the mashed bean-curd and mix well.

Leave to cook gently together for 5-6 minutes. Add remainder of stock blended with cornflour, and increase heat to high. Stir and mix together for 1 minute and serve with plain boiled rice, vegetable rice or rice gruel. *Serves 6-7.*

4 Deep-fried Tou Fu with bacon, stir-fried eggs, mushrooms and sweet peppers

4 cakes Tou Fu
4 eggs
1 teaspoon salt
225 gr (½ lb) mushrooms
3-4 rashers of bacon
2 peppers (1 red)
1 chicken stock cube
3 dl (½ pint) stock
1 tablespoon cornflour
oil for deep-frying
3 tablespoons lard or margarine
3 tablespoons soya sauce

Cut each piece of bean-curd into six. Beat eggs lightly with salt. Clean and cut mushrooms into quarters (discard stalks). Cut bacon into shreds. Deseed and cut peppers in 1·25-cm (½-in) slices. Dissolve stock cube in stock and blend with cornflour.

Deep-fry bean-curd for 3 minutes and drain. Stir-fry beaten eggs in a small frying pan and when set break up into 1·25-cm (½-in) pieces. Heat lard in a large frying pan. Add peppers, bacon and mushrooms and stir-fry over high heat for 3 minutes. Add bean-curd and eggs, mix and cook for a further 2 minutes. Pour in the meat stock blended with cornflour. Add soya sauce and stir until the liquid thickens. Leave to cook gently for 2 minutes. Can be eaten with any rice dish. *Serves 6-7.*

5 Ma Po Tou Fu (or hot mashed bean-curd with minced meat of Szechuan)

This is a very well known bean-curd dish from West China, which appeals greatly to all those who enjoy hot-tasting foods.

1 chicken stock cube
3 dl (½ pint) stock
1 tablespoon cornflour
5 cakes Tou Fu
150 gr (6 oz) Chinese (or any other) dried mushrooms
2-3 small chilli peppers (or 2 teaspoons Tabasco)
2 slices root ginger
3 tablespoons vegetable oil
2 medium onions, finely sliced
2 cloves garlic, crushed
225 gr (½ lb) minced meat
4 tablespoons soya sauce
3 tablespoons lard
2 tablespoons sherry

Dissolve stock cube in the stock. Blend well half the stock with the cornflour. Cut bean-curd into small pieces. Soak mushrooms for 20 minutes in a cup of hot water (retain water) and chop chilli pepper into thin shreds, discarding pips. Crush ginger into small grains.

Heat oil in a large saucepan. Add onions, peppers, ginger and garlic. Stir-fry them together over medium heat for 2 minutes. Add meat and stir-fry contents together over high heat for 3 minutes. Add mushrooms, mushroom water, bean-curd, soya sauce, lard and half the stock. Bring to boil and simmer for 10 minutes, stirring now and then.

Pour in the stock/cornflour mixture and sherry to mix and blend with the other ingredients. Stir and mix until the liquid has thickened. Leave to simmer over low heat for 3-4 minutes.

To be eaten with any rice dish. *Serves 6-7.*

6 Curried Tou Fu with eggs, tomatoes and potatoes

Repeat the previous recipe, but instead of chilli add 2-3 tablespoons curry powder or paste to stir-fry with onion, etc., at the beginning of cooking and a little later with the minced meat. And instead of mushrooms, use 4 eggs and 550 gr (1¼ lb) potatoes; hard-boil the eggs and cut each into 8-10 pieces, and boil potatoes for 15 minutes and cut into 2·5-cm (1-in) cubes. Add all to the curried minced meat and onion, along with the bean-curd and 1 teaspoon salt. Stir and leave to simmer gently together for 10 minutes. Finally pour in the stock/cornflour mixture. Turn the contents over a few times. Leave to simmer gently for 2-3 minutes.

Can be eaten on its own, or with any rice dish. *Serves 5-6.*

7 Tou Fu with fish in cheese sauce

This is an interesting experiment in putting together two staple foods, of East and West (bean-curd and cheese), combining them into an inexpensive, self-contained dish.

225 gr (½ lb) fillets fish	3 rashers bacon
225 gr (½ lb) potatoes	3 hard-boiled eggs
5 tablespoons butter	4 cakes Tou Fu
225 gr (½ lb) grated cheese	4 tablespoons flour

6 dl (1 pint) milk
4 tablespoons vegetable oil
3 medium onions, finely sliced
325 gr (¾ lb) cooked rice
225 gr (½ lb) cooked peas
salt and pepper to taste

Boil the fish for 5-6 minutes and flake with a fork. Boil potatoes until tender and mash with 1 tablespoon butter, half the fish and a quarter of the cheese. Cut bacon into shreds and chop hard-boiled eggs and bean-curd into small pieces. Make cheese sauce by melting 2 tablespoons butter in a saucepan and stirring in flour. Very gradually add the milk, stirring continuously over low heat. When the sauce has thickened, remove from heat and stir in balance of grated cheese.

Heat oil in a frying pan, stir-fry onion and bacon in the oil for 2 minutes. Add cooked rice, eggs, bean-curd and flaked fish. Stir-fry them together for 3-4 minutes over medium heat.

Pack the fried rice mixture at the bottom of a large deep-sided heatproof dish. Pour in the cheese sauce over the contents. Mix mashed potato and remainder of the flaked fish with salt, pepper, 2 tablespoons butter, and peas. Put a layer of this potato/fish/peas mixture on top of the cheese sauce-covered fried rice. Insert the heatproof dish into a moderate oven (180°C, 350°F, gas 4) for 20-25 minutes.

This is a complete dish, which requires no further bulk food to go with it. *Serves 5-6.*

Plain-cooked food tossed in soya sauce

People who are experienced in the use of soya sauce will immediately appreciate the difference between using soya sauce to cook with, and sprinkling it on to plain dishes after they are cooked. The improvement is very marked; soya sauce can almost invariably give dishes a character and interest they often lack when served plain.

In China, we combine soya sauce with a small amount of chopped chives, vegetable oil, shredded ginger, crushed and chopped garlic, sesame oil and a drop or two of chilli sauce. Indeed, some of the great dishes of Chinese cuisine – especially those of Mongolian-Moslem origin – are plain-cooked, the condiments and soya sauce being added by the diners themselves.

This is an important factor in Cheap Chow, as plain-cooked food often requires some added booster to fulfil the 'expanding savouriness' that is an integral part of the Chinese concept of good food.

1 Plain boiled chicken with cabbage, sprinkled with blended soya sauce

½ chicken
1·35 kg (3 lb) cabbage
2-3 slices root ginger
1 teaspoon salt
2 chicken stock cubes
450 gr (1 lb) noodles or Italian pasta

For blended soya sauce

3 tablespoons soya sauce
1½ tablespoons vegetable oil
1 tablespoon sesame oil
3 teaspoons chopped chives (or spring onion)
2 teaspoons crushed root ginger
2-3 garlic cloves, crushed
pepper to taste

Clean chicken thoroughly, including liver (cut latter into quarters). Cut cabbage into 5-cm (2-in) slices. Blend together ingredients for sauce.

Place chicken, ginger and salt in a large saucepan and cover with water. Bring to boil and simmer over low heat for 30 minutes. Skim away impurities. Simmer for a further 30 minutes. Insert cabbage under chicken. Add stock cubes and cook gently for 15 minutes. Add noodles or Italian pasta and leave to cook for a further 15 minutes.

Lift chicken out of the pan. Drain and cut meat from the bone and slice into small pieces.

Spread a quarter of the cabbage on a serving dish, as a base, and arrange the pieces of chicken on top. Sprinkle the blended soya sauce over the chicken.

Divide the cabbage and noodles and a proportion of soup into bowls for individual diners. Serve the dish of chicken and cabbage at the centre of the table and diners can help themselves from it. *Serves 5-6.*

2 Plain-cooked turkey and cabbage sprinkled with blended soya sauce

When in season (around Christmas-time) turkey can be cheap, and only a quarter of a bird should be sufficient if prepared as in the previous recipe. Turkey, being a slightly tougher bird than chicken, requires 1½ hours of simmering, before the cabbage is added for the final 30 minutes of cooking. As it is also a stronger-tasting meat, add a double portion of sliced root ginger (4-5 slices) into the cooking from the beginning.

An alternative way of serving is to separate the cabbage from the meat and soup. The cabbage should be stirred in 2-3 tablespoons of chicken or turkey fat over a high heat for a couple of minutes and served on a separate dish. In this case, only noodles are served in the soup itself in the diners' individual bowls. They then help themselves from the two dishes of turkey and cabbage served at the centre of the table. *Serves 5-6.*

3 Plain-cooked pork and cabbage sprinkled with blended soya sauce

The advantage of this dish is that almost any cut of pork is suitable, or even a combination of cuts (hand, spring, shanks, blade, belly, shoulder, spare-ribs, etc.).

1·35 kg (3 lb) pork (with bones)
3 slices root ginger
1 large cabbage
salt and pepper to taste
675 gr (1½ lb) noodles (or Italian pasta)
3 tablespoons butter

For blended soya sauce
Prepare blended soya sauce in the same manner as in recipe 1, but add 1 teaspoon chilli sauce and increase ingredients employed by an all-round 50 per cent.

Place pork and ginger in 3 litres (5 pints) of water in a large pot, saucepan or casserole. Bring to the boil and simmer over a low heat for 1 hour. Skim away fat and impurities. Simmer for a further 1 hour. Insert cabbage, sliced into 5-cm (2-in) pieces, under the pork, bring to the boil and simmer together for another 20 minutes. Add the noodles or Italian pasta, season with salt, and simmer for a further 15 minutes.

Remove pork from pan. Drain, cut meat from bone into neat slices. Arrange on a serving dish and sprinkle with 50-60 per cent of the blended soya sauce. Remove and drain cabbage (drain into the pot). Then toss cabbage in 3 tablespoons butter in a large frying pan over high heat for 3 minutes. Sprinkle with the balance of blended soya sauce and pepper and serve on separate dishes.

Divide the soup and noodles into individual bowls and serve as noodle soup. This three-dish combination is served with bulk food. *Serves 8-10.*

4 Plain-boiled mutton (or lamb) with cabbage sprinkled with blended soya sauce

Mutton or lamb can be cooked as in the previous recipe. In Peking there are many well-known Chinese-Moslem restaurants where mutton and lamb are cooked slowly; they are sometimes then quick-fried just before cutting into neat slices for serving. In Chinese cooking of mutton or lamb, the addition of sliced root ginger is almost obligatory, and often a liberal addition of wine (or beer) in the last stages of cooking is recommended. *Serves 8-10.*

5 Plain-boiled beef with cabbage sprinkled with blended soya sauce

Beef can be plain-boiled in precisely the same manner as pork in recipe 3, except that it should be cooked over even lower heat for 1 hour longer. As with mutton or lamb, 2-3 slices of ginger are usually added at the beginning; and a few carrots (sliced diagonally) may also be added to cook with the cabbage. Again, a variety of cuts of beef can be used, and, since in the end the meat is cut off the bones into neat pieces, its original form does not really matter.

Another advantage of very long, slow cooking is that the fat will end up highly palatable (and no longer greasy), especially when sprinkled with soya sauce or blended soya sauce. Beef cooked in this manner can be served as a three-dish combination: sliced beef sprinkled with blended soya sauce, beef noodle soup, cabbage and carrots tossed in butter and spiced with salt, pepper and soya sauce. *Serves 6–8.*

6 Plain-boiled fish tossed in blended soya sauce with leeks, bean-sprouts and noodles

One of the distinctive aspects of Chinese fish cookery is that fish is often cooked in meat or chicken broth. The stock becomes fish-flavoured, but the fish retains its freshness and purity, so long as it is not over-cooked. Any fishiness that may be present in the stock is counteracted by the addition of ginger, garlic and wine at an early stage. The fish is flaked into small pieces and tossed or sprinkled with blended soya sauce.

3 rashers bacon
150 gr (6 oz) leeks
550 gr (1¼ lb) fish (cod, haddock, halibut, bass, mullet, shad, pike, etc.)
1·5 litres (2½ pints) stock
1 teaspoon salt
2 chicken stock cubes
2-3 slices root ginger
450 gr (1 lb) noodles (or spaghetti)
450 gr (1 lb) bean-sprouts

For blended soya sauce

3 tablespoons soya sauce
2 teaspoons chopped root ginger
1 tablespoon vegetable oil
2 teaspoons sesame oil
1 tablespoon chopped spring onion
½ teaspoon sugar
1 tablespoon sherry
1 tablespoon vinegar

Blend ingredients for the sauce in a bowl. Shred bacon, clean and cut leeks diagonally into 2·5-cm (1-in) segments. Clean and de-gut the fish (this can be done by fishmongers).

Heat stock in a large saucepan or casserole. Add salt, stock cubes, ginger, leeks and bring to the boil. Simmer for 4-5 minutes. Add the fish and continue to cook gently for 9-10 minutes. Remove fish from the stock and flake (first removing and discarding bones, head, etc.). Arrange on a flat serving dish and sprinkle with blended soya sauce.

Meanwhile add shredded bacon and noodles into the stock. Bring to the boil and simmer for 10 minutes. Add the sprouts and simmer for another 7-8 minutes. Adjust seasoning. Divide the noodles, sprouts, etc. into 5-6 bowls and serve, to be eaten in conjunction with the fish, which should be placed at the centre of the table. *Serves 5-6.*

7 Boiled eggs tossed in blended soya sauce with peas and spring onions

6-8 eggs
3-4 stalks spring onion
450 gr (1 lb) green peas
3 tablespoons butter
4-5 tablespoons blended soya sauce (prepared as in the previous recipe)

Hard-boil the eggs. Remove shells and cut each egg neatly into six segments. Cut spring onions into 2·5-cm (1-in) segments.

Heat peas in a small saucepan with 3 tablespoons butter (or margarine) for 3-4 minutes. Arrange the pieces of eggs on a large serving dish. Spread the peas around them. Sprinkle with spring onions and blended soya sauce.

Serve the dish cold, surrounded by bowls of hot congee (rice-gruel). In China, this would be considered a very satisfying breakfast or midnight supper. *Serves 5-6.*

12 Rice and noodle salads and Chinese jellied meats

Salads

In Chinese cold-tossed rice and noodle dishes, the supplementary ingredients are cut into pieces similar in size to that of the accompanying bulk food – for rice into grains, and for noodles into matchstick strips.

1 Chinese rice salad A

½ chicken stock cube
4-5 tablespoons concentrated chicken stock
4-5 eggs
225 gr (½ lb) young carrots
1 medium can button mushrooms
3 tablespoons vegetable oil
3 tablespoons butter
225 gr (½ lb) frozen peas
225 gr (½ lb) canned sweet corn
550 gr (1¼ lb) cooked rice
3 stalks spring onions, sliced
3 tablespoons soya sauce
1 tablespoon vinegar
2 tablespoons sesame oil

Dissolve the stock cube in stock (stir until wholly dissolved). Hard-boil the eggs and chop roughly. Clean the carrots and chop roughly. Drain canned mushrooms.

Heat oil and butter in a saucepan. Add carrots and cook for 2 minutes over medium heat. Add mushrooms and peas and cook for a further 3 minutes. Add corn and mix. Heat for 1 more minute, then add into the rice, together with the chopped eggs. Toss lightly together.

Blend the spring onions, soya sauce, vinegar and sesame oil in a bowl and sprinkle over the rice. Serve hot or cold. *Serves 4-5.*

2 Chinese rice salad B

½ medium-size cucumber
225 gr (½ lb) heart of cabbage
2 medium sweet peppers
225 gr (½ lb) braised bamboo shoots (canned)
4 hard-boiled eggs
225 gr (½ lb) beetroot
3-4 stalks spring onions
5 tablespoons vegetable oil
2 garlic cloves, crushed
225 gr (½ lb) bean-sprouts
4-5 tablespoons sultanas
550 gr (1¼ lb) cooked rice
1½ tablespoons parsley
2 tablespoons sherry
5-6 tablespoons blended soya sauce (see page 129)

Cut the cucumber (including skin), cabbage, deseeded peppers, bamboo shoots, eggs and beetroot into large-sultana-size pieces. Cut spring onions into 1·25-cm (½-in) slices.

Heat vegetable oil in a large saucepan. Add peppers, cabbage and garlic and stir over high heat for 2 minutes. Add bean-sprouts, sultanas and bamboo shoots and continue to stir for 2 more minutes. Pour into the rice and toss lightly. Finally, add chopped eggs, spring onion, cucumber and beetroot and mix together.

Just before serving, sprinkle the rice mixture with parsley, sherry and blended soya sauce. This Chinese rice salad is suitable for eating on its own, or it can be consumed hot or cold with meat, poultry or fish in aspic dishes (see pages 138–42). *Serves 5-6.*

3 Chinese noodle salad A

1 chicken stock cube
225 gr (½ lb) celery
3 slices root ginger
1 sweet pepper, deseeded
225 gr (½ lb) cooked meat
3-4 stalks spring onions
450 gr (1 lb) bean-sprouts
550 gr (1¼ lb) noodles or Italian pasta
6 tablespoons vegetable oil
1½ teaspoons salt

For blended soya sauce

4 tablespoons soya sauce
1 tablespoon vinegar
1 teaspoon chilli sauce
2 tablespoons sherry
1½ teaspoons sugar
1 tablespoon sesame oil

Dissolve the stock cube in 4-5 tablespoons hot water. Cut celery, ginger and pepper and cooked meat into large-noodle-size matchstick shreds, and spring onions into 1·25-cm (½-in) segments. Wash sprouts and drain thoroughly. Boil noodles for 5 minutes or pasta for 10 minutes and drain. Rinse under running water.

Heat 5 tablespoons oil in a large saucepan. Add celery, ginger and peppers and stir-fry over high heat for 2 minutes. Add sprouts, spring onions and salt and continue to stir-fry for 3 minutes. Add all ingredients, including shredded cooked meat, to the noodles or pasta and toss gently together.

Blend stock, soya sauce, vinegar, chilli sauce, sherry, sugar, sesame oil and remainder of vegetable oil into a sauce. Sprinkle over noodle salad and toss again lightly. *Serves 5-6.*

4 Chinese noodle salad B

550 gr (1¼ lb) noodles or spaghetti
225 gr (½ lb) young leeks
½ medium cucumber
225 gr (½ lb) mushrooms
4-5 stalks spring onions
4-5 medium tomatoes
5 tablespoons vegetable oil
225 gr (½ lb) bean-sprouts
2 teaspoons salt
1½ tablespoons sesame oil
1½ tablespoons chopped parsley
1½ tablespoons vinegar
blended soya sauce (see previous recipe)

Boil noodles or pasta for 5 or 10 minutes respectively. Drain and rinse under running water. Cut leeks, cucumber (including skin), and mushroom caps (discard stalks) into double matchstick shreds. Cut spring onions into 1·25-cm (½-in) segments. Cut each tomato into 6 wedges.

Heat vegetable oil in a large saucepan. Add leeks, mushrooms. Stir-fry them together over high heat for 3 minutes. Add sprouts, tomatoes, cucumber and salt and continue to stir-fry over high heat for 3 minutes. Add the vegetables to the noodles or pasta and toss lightly.

Sprinkle with sesame oil, parsley and vinegar in addition to the blended soya sauce. Toss lightly together again. *Serves 5-6*.

Chinese jellied meats

It is very much in the Chinese tradition to produce 'jellied meats', if only because bones and skin are included in the cooking, with the result that almost any of the long-simmered or red-cooked dishes will jellify if left to cool. Besides, jellied meats are very much in keeping with the Chinese concept of 'expanding savouriness'.

Jellied meat dishes can be made quite elaborate by clarifying the stock used, and embedding in the clear jelly particular leaves of vegetables, cuts of meat, or even flowers. A small amount of gelatine added to the stock makes the preparation that much simpler and more certain.

In Chinese cooking, the flavour of such dishes is usually amplified by the addition of concentrated chicken stock, soya sauce, wine, sugar, chopped chives and a small amount of ginger.

Jellied meat dishes are naturally economical, as the meat used is often taken from the cheaper cuts.

1 Pig's trotters and belly of pork in aspic

2 pairs of trotters
450 gr (1 lb) belly of pork (with skin)
4 stalks spring onions
1·8 litres (3 pints) water
2 teaspoons salt
4 tablespoons soya sauce
2 chicken stock cubes
2-3 teaspoons sugar
1·5 dl ($\frac{1}{4}$ pint) wine (red or white)
pepper to taste
1$\frac{1}{2}$ tablespoons gelatine

Clean the trotters thoroughly. Cut belly of pork through skin into small strips (the length being the depth of the lean and fat). Cut spring onions into 2·5-cm (1-in) segments.

Bring water to boil in a large saucepan or casserole. Add trotters, salt and pork. Bring to boil and simmer for 30 minutes. Skim away impurities. Insert an asbestos sheet under the casserole and leave to simmer over very low heat for 1 hour. Add soya sauce, stock cubes, sugar and half the wine, and continue to simmer for 1 more hour.

Remove trotters from the stock. Scrape the meat and skin from bone (discard latter) and return the former into the pan. Add pepper, gelatine and balance of wine. Simmer and stir contents for 5-6 minutes. Turn off heat and sprinkle contents with chopped spring onions. When somewhat cooler, skim surface for fat and pour the contents into a large deep-sided dish and insert the latter into the refrigerator for 2½-3 hours.

After 2½-3 hours' cooling in the refrigerator, the liquid in the dish will have become firm and well set. One can either serve the pork and trotters in aspic in the original dish, or turn out on to a large serving dish. Serve plain, or decorate with some crisp lettuce leaves and tomatoes. To be eaten with congee, vegetable rice, fried rice, in the winter, or rice salad or noodle salad, in the summer. *Serves 6-8.*

2 Calf's foot and shin of beef in aspic

1 pair calf's feet
450 gr (1 lb) shin of beef
225 gr (½ lb) carrots
225 gr (½ lb) turnips
4 stalks spring onions
1·8 litres (3 pints) water
2 teaspoons salt
pepper to taste
3-4 slices root ginger
2 chicken stock cubes
4 tablespoons soya sauce
2 teaspoons sugar
2 tablespoons gelatine
1·5 dl (¼ pint) wine (red or white)

Scrape and clean calf's feet thoroughly. Cut beef into 2·5-cm (1-in) cubes. Clean and cut carrots and turnips diagonally into 2·5-cm (1-in) segments. Chop spring onions into 1·25-cm (½-in) segments.

Place calf's feet and beef in large heavy pan or casserole. Add water, bring to the boil, and simmer for 30 minutes. Skim away impurities. Insert an asbestos sheet under the pan. Add salt, pepper and ginger. Leave to simmer very gently for 1½ hours. Again, skim away impurities. Remove calf's feet from pan. Scrape and cut meat from bones (discard bones). Return meat into pan. Add stock cubes, soya sauce, sugar, carrots and turnips. Leave to simmer for 30 minutes. Stir in the gelatine and wine. Leave to cook for 10 minutes. Add spring onions and simmer for a further 5 minutes. Remove from heat. When somewhat cooler, pour the contents into a large, deep-sided serving dish. Put the dish into the refrigerator for 2½-3 hours, for the contents to set.

Serve as in the previous recipe. *Serves 6-8.*

3 Neck of mutton in aspic

2 medium onions
1 bunch watercress
1·35 kg (3 lb) neck of mutton (with bones)
2·4 litres (4 pints) water
3-4 slices root ginger
2 garlic cloves, crushed
4 tablespoons soya sauce
2 teaspoons salt
pepper to taste
2 chicken stock cubes
6 dl (1 pint) wine (red or white)
2 tablespoons gelatine

Quarter the onions and coarsely chop watercress (discarding roots). Place mutton and water in a large pot or casserole. Bring to the boil and simmer gently for 45 minutes. Skim away fat and impurities. Add ginger, garlic, onion, soya sauce, salt and pepper. Insert an asbestos sheet under container and simmer gently for 1½ hours. Lift mutton out of pot. Add stock cubes, wine, gelatine and watercress to pot, and simmer and stir for 10 minutes. Scrape meat from bones and return it into the pot. Remove pot from heat and leave contents to cool for 30 minutes, then pour into a deep-sided serving dish. When somewhat cooler, place dish in the refrigerator for 3 hours, for the contents to set.

As well as being eaten with hot rice and noodles (or with rice and noodle salad), this dish is often, in China, used as an accompaniment to wine and drinks. *Serves 6-8.*

4 Chicken in aspic

½ chicken (approximately 675 gr or 1½ lb)
2·4 litres (4 pints) water
2 teaspoons salt
3 slices root ginger
225 gr (½ lb) young carrots
550 gr (1¼ lb) cauliflower
2 chicken stock cubes
3 dl (½ pint) white wine
2 tablespoons gelatine
3 firm tomatoes
3 stalks spring onions

Place chicken and water in a large heavy saucepan or casserole. Bring to the boil and add salt and ginger. Simmer for 45 minutes and skim away fat and impurities. Clean carrots and cut diagonally into 2·5-cm (1-in) segments and add them into the pan.

Continue to cook gently for 30 minutes. Break cauliflower into small individual florets and add them into the pan and cook for a further 15 minutes. Lift the chicken out of the pan and scrape the meat from the bones. Cut meat into even-sized pieces and return to the soup, together with the stock cubes, wine and gelatine. Stir for 5 minutes over low heat. Cut tomatoes into quarters and spring onions into 3·75-cm (1½-in) segments and add them, too, to the soup. Stir a few times, turn heat off and leave contents to cool.

When cool, arrange the pieces of chicken, cauliflower, tomatoes, etc. evenly over the bottom of a deep-sided serving dish. Strain, or double strain, the soup into the dish. Place in the refrigerator for 3 hours to set.

As the stock has been well strained the meat jelly should be quite clear and the pieces of cauliflower, chicken and carrots clearly visible. The dish should be attractive, and suitable for parties. It can be eaten with hot rice, noodles, or rice salad, etc. *Serves 5-6.*

5 Fish in aspic

Fish in aspic can be one of the cheapest dishes, if only because fish tails and heads can be obtained here for next to nothing. Although in China they are sometimes prized as delicacies, it would cause amazement in the West if one offered guests a meal of nothing but fish tails and heads. In this recipe I have, therefore, included 450 gr (1 lb) filleted white fish.

1 kg (2¼ lb) fish tails and heads	2 garlic cloves, crushed
450 gr (1 lb) white fish	2 teaspoons salt
2 onions	2·4 litres (4 pints) water
3 medium tomatoes	2 chicken stock cubes
3 stalks spring onions	1 glass white wine
4 slices root ginger	2 tablespoons gelatine

Wash fish tails and heads thoroughly. Cut white fish into small pieces. Cut onions and tomatoes into quarters. Cut spring onions into 2·5-cm (1-in) segments.

Place fish heads and tails with ginger, garlic, onion, salt and water in a saucepan. Bring to the boil and simmer gently for 1¼ hours. Add stock cubes and simmer for a further 30 minutes.

Strain through double layers of muslin. Pour the stock into a clean pan. Add fish, spring onions, tomatoes, wine and gelatine. Bring to the boil and simmer gently for 5 minutes. Transfer contents to a large Pyrex dish to cool. When cold place dish in the refrigerator for 3 hours to set.

When set, turn out on to a large dish and serve cut into slices, with hot or cold rice dishes. *Serves 5-6.*

13 Cheese dishes

When writing about Chinese cooking, one is too inclined to dismiss cheese, but in Cheap Chow dishes, cheese can be very useful. There are probably many points in Chinese culinary creations where it can be introduced to advantage.

1 Stir-fried eggs on fried bread with grated cheese and chopped spring onions

4 eggs
1 teaspoon salt
3 stalks spring onions
2 tablespoons vegetable oil
1½ tablespoons margarine
4 thick slices bread
3 tablespoons butter
6 tablespoons grated cheese
pepper to taste

Beat eggs and salt with a fork for 8-10 seconds. Slice spring onions into 1·25-cm (½-in) segments. Add half of these into the beaten egg and mix well.

Heat oil and margarine in a frying pan and fry bread for 2

minutes on one side and 1½ minutes on the other. Remove from the pan.

Melt butter in frying pan, then pour in beaten egg. When about to set, stir egg around gently a couple of times. Divide into 4 portions and spread evenly on top of the drier (under-fried) side of each slice of bread. Sprinkle with grated cheese, pepper and the balance of spring onions. Place under the grill for 2-2½ minutes until cheese is lightly browned. *Serves 4.*

2 Stir-fried eggs on fried bread with spinach, grated cheese and tomatoes

This is really a variation on the theme of the previous recipe; here, the colourful and nourishing vegetables make a better-balanced and more attractive dish.

Repeat the previous recipe, but use in addition 2 medium sized tomatoes and 225 gr (½ lb) spinach. Cut tomatoes into slices, and remove tough parts of the spinach. After having fried the bread and stir-fried the eggs, spread the latter on top of the bread. Use an extra 1½ tablespoons vegetable oil and 1½ tablespoons margarine or butter to stir-fry the spinach over a high heat for 2 minutes. Spread the spinach and tomatoes on top of the eggs. Sprinkle with grated cheese and place under the grill for 2-2½ minutes. *Serves 4.*

3 Stir-fried minced meat with bean-curd on fried bread with grated cheese

Here a typical Chinese food (bean-curd) is used in conjunction with stir-fried meat to provide interest and added nourishment to bread.

2 stalks spring onions
2 cakes bean-curd
3 tablespoons butter or margarine
4 slices bread
3 tablespoons vegetable oil
1 tablespoon butter
(or sesame oil)
150 gr (6 oz) minced meat
½ teaspoon salt
pepper to taste
1½ tablespoons soya sauce
6 tablespoons grated cheese

Cut spring onions into 1·25-cm (½-in) segments. Cut each cake of bean-curd into a dozen pieces.

Heat butter or margarine in a frying pan. Fry both sides of the bread – 2 minutes on the first side and 1½ minutes on the second.

Heat oil and butter in another frying pan. Add minced meat, salt and pepper and stir-fry over high heat for 3 minutes. Add bean-curd and soya sauce. Mash these with the minced meat and stir-fry together for 2 minutes; reduce heat and leave to cook for 2 minutes more.

'Butter' the slices of bread with this meat-cum-bean-curd mixture. Sprinkle with chopped spring onion and grated cheese. Place these 'Chinese open sandwiches' under the grill for 2-2½ minutes. *Serves 4.*

4 Stir-fried vegetables on fried bread with grated cheese

100 gr (4 oz) young carrots	100 gr (4 oz) bean-sprouts
100 gr (4 oz) small cucumber	½ teaspoon salt
1 bunch watercress	1 tablespoon soya sauce
4 thick slices bread	½ teaspoon sugar
3 tablespoons vegetable oil	¾ teaspoon mustard powder
1 tablespoon butter	6 tablespoons grated cheese

Clean and shred carrots and cucumber into fine matchstick shreds. Remove lower stems and roots of watercress and chop coarsely. Fry bread as in previous recipe.

Heat oil and butter in a large frying pan until very hot. Add all the vegetables and stir-fry over high heat for 3 minutes, adding salt, soya sauce, sugar and mustard. Divide the vegetables into 4 portions and spread each on top of a slice of fried bread. Sprinkle the top of the vegetables with grated cheese. Place under the grill for 2-2½ minutes.

This vegetarian snack is savoury enough to appeal to meat eaters. *Serves 4.*

5 Stir-fried vegetables and shredded meat on fried bread with grated cheese

For inveterate meat eaters, the previous recipe can be converted into a meat dish simply by adding some shredded meat into the stir-frying of the vegetables. Almost any meat can be used, and should be put into the pan to stir-fry 1 minute before the vegetables are added (pork should be added 2 minutes before the vegetables). If cooked meats are used, they can simply be shredded and added into the stir-frying with the vegetables.

This mixed dish is best kept fairly dry – without too much gravy, which might soak into and spoil the texture of the fried bread underneath. *Serves 4.*

Grated cheese and cheese sauce

These two cheese ingredients can be used together with great effect on cooked rice, especially when some typical Chinese ingredients are also incorporated. In other words, this is another case where the advantages of Eastern and Western methods and ingredients can be combined to produce another series of highly acceptable Cheap Chow dishes.

1 Baked rice with cheese sauce, egg, chopped bacon and grated cheese

4 hard-boiled eggs
1 large onion
3 rashers bacon
2 firm medium tomatoes
3 stalks spring onions
2 tablespoons vegetable oil
675 gr (1½ lb) boiled rice
1 teaspoon salt
4-5 tablespoons grated cheese

For cheese sauce

5-6 heaped tablespoons margarine or butter
5-6 heaped tablespoons flour
salt and pepper to taste
3 dl (½ pint) milk
6 heaped tablespoons grated cheese

Prepare the cheese sauce by stirring the butter or margarine with the flour in a saucepan for 3-4 minutes over low heat until they form into a thick roux. Add salt, pepper and pour in the milk in a thin stream, stirring all the time until a smooth sauce is obtained. Follow by adding and folding in the grated cheese slowly, again stirring all the time, still over a low heat, for about 2 minutes.

Finely chop the hard-boiled eggs, onion and bacon. Cut tomatoes into slices and spring onions into 2·5-cm (1-in) segments. Stir-fry chopped bacon and onion in the vegetable oil for 3 minutes. Add to the rice, together with salt and hard-boiled eggs. Mix all lightly together. Pack into a deep-sided heatproof dish (or casserole). Pour the cheese sauce over the rice, making holes in the rice at regular intervals, so that the sauce will sink into it. Cover with sliced tomatoes and sprinkle with grated cheese and spring onions. Then finish by placing in a pre-heated oven, 180°C, 350°F, gas 4, for 15 minutes. *Serves 4-5.*

2 Baked rice with bacon, mushrooms, cucumber, cheese sauce and grated cheese

Repeat the previous recipe, but instead of using hard-boiled eggs use half a cucumber and 225 gr (½ lb) chopped mushrooms (or small button mushrooms). Stir-fry mushrooms in 2 tablespoons vegetable oil and 1 tablespoon of butter for 3 minutes and mix into the rice.

To prepare the cheese sauce, chop cucumber into 1·25-cm (½-in) cubes, and fold these into the sauce. After packing the rice, etc. into a deep-sided heatproof dish (or casserole) pour the sauce with the cucumber evenly over the rice. Sprinkle with grated cheese and chopped spring onions.

Place the dish or casserole in a pre-heated oven set at 180°C, 350°F, gas 4, for 15 minutes. *Serves 4-5.*

3 Smoked or fresh fish and fried rice with cheese sauce and grated cheese

2 hard-boiled eggs
325 gr (¾ lb) smoked haddock or fresh fish (cod, etc.)
salt and pepper
2 rashers bacon
3 tablespoons vegetable oil
2 tablespoons butter or margarine
2 medium onions, finely sliced
675 gr (1½ lb) cooked rice
2 stalks spring onions
3 sprays watercress
cheese sauce (prepared as on page 146)
6 heaped tablespoons grated cheese

Chop hard-boiled eggs finely. Parboil fish for 5-6 minutes, and flake with a fork. Season liberally with salt and pepper. Shred bacon finely.

Heat oil and butter in a frying pan. Add onion and bacon and stir-fry over a high heat for 2 minutes. Reduce heat. Add fish and egg, and mix. Add to the rice and mix lightly together. Pack the mixture into a deep-sided heatproof dish (or casserole).

Chop watercress coarsely. Pour the cheese sauce evenly over the rice, etc. in the heatproof dish. Sprinkle with grated cheese, shredded spring onion and chopped watercress. Place the dish in a pre-heated oven set at 180°C, 350°F, gas 4, for 15 minutes. *Serves 4-5.*

Noodles with cheese sauce and grated cheese

All the three previous recipes, which are prepared with rice, can just as well be prepared with noodles or Italian pasta.

14 Sweet dishes

Among the cheaper Chinese sweet dishes, there is a whole series prepared by using congee (rice-gruel) as the base. A variety of dried and fresh fruits (whichever are available) can be added. The congee is first of all sweetened with sugar, and if you have any syrup from canned fruits pour that in too. Fresh fruits should be peeled and diced into approximately 1·25-cm (½-in) pieces, wedged or cubed, but they require only very short cooking, probably no more than 5-10 minutes of simmering over a low heat. A small amount of colourful crystallized fruits, such as maraschino cherries and glacé fruit, may be added. This series of sweet dishes can suitably be called 'Chinese rice puddings'.

Among these rice pudding dishes the one which is the most popular in China consists of simply cooking together rice with Chinese red beans, and adding into it a reasonable quantity of brown sugar. Although this is a very simple product, and is usually served in the afternoons rather than towards the end of a meal, it is probably twice as warming and comforting as hot tea.

1 Chinese red-bean rice-gruel

225 gr (8 oz) Chinese red beans
1·8 litres (3 pints) water
150-175 gr (6-7 oz) rice (brown or glutinous)
4-5 tablespoons brown sugar

Soak red beans in water overnight and drain.

Place red beans and rice at the bottom of a heavy pan. Add water, bring to boil. Insert an asbestos sheet under the pan and reduce heat to a very low simmer.

Simmer for 1½ hours, stirring with a wooden spoon every now and then. Add sugar, and simmer for another 30 minutes, stirring every 5 minutes.

Serve in individual bowls (like porridge). When there is little or nothing else much to eat, two bowls of this 'porridge' can be a meal in itself. *Serves 4.*

2 Chinese chopped-date rice-gruel

The procedure in preparing this dish is largely the same as for the previous recipe, except that Chinese red dates are substituted for Chinese red beans. But the dates require a considerably shorter cooking than the beans: 15-20 minutes at most.

225-250 gr (8-9 oz) Chinese red dates
1·8 litres (3 pints) water
150-175 gr (6-7 oz) rice (glutinous or brown)
4-5 heaped tablespoons sugar

Wash dates and place in saucepan with water. Bring to boil and simmer for 25 minutes. Skin and pit dates, and chop roughly. Prepare rice-gruel by heating and simmering rice in 1·8 litres (3 pints) water for 1¾ hours.

Add dates and sugar to rice-gruel. Heat together gently and simmer for 15-20 minutes, stirring now and then.

Serve in individual bowls. This rice pudding is lighter and smoother than that in the previous recipe. *Serves 4.*

3 Chinese tangerine (or orange) rice-gruel

150-175 gr (6-7 oz) rice (glutinous or brown)
1·8 litres (3 pints) water
2-3 medium/large oranges or tangerines
4-5 heaped tablespoons sugar

Prepare the rice-gruel as in recipe 1, above. Peel and chop the oranges into half segments and add to the rice-gruel along with the sugar. Heat gently together for 10-15 minutes.

This dessert can be served hot or well chilled. When five or more portions are required, a small can (225 gr or 8 oz) of mandarins in syrup can be added into the rice-gruel-and-oranges. *Serves 4.*

4 Chinese pear and prune rice-gruel

Pears and prunes are used together here because of their colour contrast and the difference in degree of sweetness.

150-175 gr (6-7 oz) rice (glutinous or brown)
1·8 litres (3 pints) water
2-3 pears
4-5 heaped tablespoons sugar
250 gr (9 oz) prunes (canned)

As in recipe 1, above, prepare the rice-gruel by simmering rice in water for 1¾ hours. Peel and core the pears, and cut into 1·25-cm (½-in) pieces. Add these to the rice-gruel along with the sugar, prunes and prune syrup. Heat and stir together gently for 5-10 minutes.

Can be eaten hot or well chilled. *Serves 4.*

5 Chinese rice pudding with fruit and nut combinations

150-175 gr (6-7 oz) glutinous rice
1·8 litres (3 pints) water
1-2 apples
4-5 heaped tablespoons sugar
3-4 tablespoons dried figs (or dried dragon's eyes)
3-4 tablespoons raisins (or sultanas)
75-100 gr (3-4 oz) coarsely chopped almonds, and/or walnuts

Prepare the rice-gruel by simmering rice in water as in recipe 1. Peel and core the apples and cut into 1·25-cm (½-in) pieces. Add these to the rice-gruel, along with the sugar, figs, raisins (and/or dragon's eyes and sultanas). Simmer together gently for 15 minutes. Add chopped almonds and walnuts and serve hot. *Serves 4.*

6 Chinese rice pudding with peaches

150-175 gr (6-7 oz) glutinous rice
1·8 litres (3 pints) water
2 large peaches
4-5 heaped tablespoons brown sugar
1 small can sliced peaches in syrup

Prepare rice-gruel as in recipe 1 (see page 150).

Peel and pit the fresh peaches and cut into thin slices. Add them to the rice pudding along with sugar and canned peaches and syrup (it may be necessary to cut the canned peaches into the same size pieces as the fresh ones).

Heat, then simmer all together for 10-15 minutes, stirring occasionally. Serve hot or well chilled. *Serves 4.*

7 Chinese rice pudding with strawberries

150-175 gr (6-7 oz) glutinous rice	4-5 heaped tablespoons sugar
1·8 litres (3 pints) water	4-5 tablespoons strawberry jam
225 gr (8 oz) fresh strawberries	1-2 tablespoons cream (optional)

Prepare rice-gruel as in recipe 1, page 150.

Clean and cut each strawberry in half. Add them to the rice pudding along with sugar. Heat the mixture through over a low heat for 5-6 minutes.

Divide rice pudding and strawberries equally into 4 bowls. Place 1 large tablespoon of strawberry jam at the centre of the pudding in each bowl (cream may also be added for those who have a fondness for creamy things) and serve either hot or chilled. *Serves 4.*

8 Chinese green pea pudding

450 gr (1 lb) dried split peas	2 tablespoons cornflour
100 gr (4 oz) glutinous rice	4-5 heaped tablespoons sugar
1·8 litres (3 pints) water	1·5 dl ($\frac{1}{4}$ pint) hot water

Soak peas overnight. Drain and place in a heavy saucepan. Add rice and water. Bring to boil, and simmer very gently with asbestos sheet under the pan, for 2 hours, stirring now and then.

Blend cornflour and sugar in hot water. Add the blended mixture into the contents of the pan. Heat gently for 5-6 minutes, stirring all the time. Pour the mixture into a rectangular pan to a depth of 2·5 cm (1 in) to cool.

When cold, put pan into a refrigerator for 2 hours, then cut 'pudding' into cubes. *Serves 4.* (In China it is usually placed on toothpicks and eaten as a candy.)

9 Sweet peanut 'tea'

In the West this dessert would be called 'peanut pudding', but in China we call it 'tea'.

325 gr ($\frac{3}{4}$ lb) unsalted peanuts
2 teaspoons baking soda
1·5 litres ($2\frac{1}{2}$ pints) water
5 tablespoons brown sugar

Place peanuts, soda, and water in a saucepan. Bring to boil, and simmer very gently for 2 hours (with asbestos sheet under the pan). Add sugar and stir for 2-3 minutes until it has completely dissolved.

Serve hot in small bowls. When food is short this 'tea' can be very strengthening, because of its heat and nourishing contents. *Serves 4.*

10 Water chestnut and fruit jelly

$1\frac{1}{2}$ tablespoons gelatine
6 dl (1 pint) water
4 tablespoons sugar
5-6 tablespoons water chestnut flour
2-3 tablespoons cornflour
225 gr ($\frac{1}{2}$ lb) water chestnuts (tinned)
2-3 slices of pineapple

Add gelatine to water. Heat gently and stir until the gelatine has completely dissolved. Add sugar, water chestnut flour and cornflour. Stir and mix until completely blended. Heat gently for a further 3-4 minutes.

Shred water chestnuts and pineapple, and place in an oval or rectangular dish. Pour the blended liquid mixture over the shredded pineapple and chestnuts and mix gently. When somewhat cool, place the dish in a refrigerator for the contents to set.

After a couple of hours, when contents have set, cut the jelly into half-a-dozen or more pieces, and serve one piece per person. The shredded pineapple and water chestnut in the jelly provide a crunchiness that gives a new dimension to the jelly. *Serves 4.*

Index

master sauce, basic 59–60
cooking with 16–17, 58–66